BREAKING THE CHAINS OF CULTURE

BUILDING TRUST IN INDIVIDUALS, TEAMS, AND ORGANIZATIONS

George Vukotich Ph. D.

Copyright © 2008 George Vukotich Ph. D.
All rights reserved.

ISBN: 1-4196-9512-6
ISBN-13: 9781419695124

Visit www.booksurge.com to order additional copies.

Dedication

This book is dedicated to all the talented individuals who have been demoralized, displaced, or had their careers negatively impacted by those who could not build trust and create positive work environments. May we all learn, may we all grow, may we all prosper.

Table of Contents

Chapter 1.	The Three Dimensions of Trust	7
Chapter 2.	Common Barriers to Building Trust	31
Chapter 3.	Why Fixing Symptoms Doesn't Solve Problems	51
Chapter 4.	How Filters and Bias impact Our Interactions with Others	65
Chapter 5.	How Handoffs, Denials, and Delegation Impact Trust	83
Chapter 6.	What Creates Trust and Distrust among Individuals	101
Chapter 7.	Why Things Don't Just Work Themselves Out	119
Chapter 8.	How Trust Impacts an Organization's Talent Base	133
Chapter 9.	Recognizing Controlling Behaviors	143
Chapter 10.	The Impact Relationships Have on an Organization's Success	163
Chapter 11.	Creating an Atmosphere of Trust	191
Chapter 12.	Expectations and Communication	203
Chapter 13.	Breaking the Chains of Culture	229
Some Final Thoughts		245

CHAPTER 1.
THE THREE DIMENSIONS OF TRUST

Chapter Goals:

- Understand how "push" and "pull" factors impact an individual's relationship with an organization.

- Understand how the dimensions of confidence, fear, and risk relate to trust.

- Understand the impact of trust in relationships.

Introduction

In working with hundreds of organizations over the past twenty years we have consistently found that one of the biggest problems holding organizations back from being successful over the long term is a lack of trust among individuals. It often starts as the result of one individual trying to reach a goal or accomplish a task, but in the process, other individuals are impacted by what may be described as *unintended consequences* that result from the individual's actions. It happens at all levels, with individuals from all backgrounds. It is not necessarily that anyone wants to do something harmful or malicious to someone else, it is that they have a self-interest and value and belief system that is focused on what has helped them be successful in the past.

Individuals, in their efforts to be successful on the job, hope that what they have done in the past will allow them to reach higher levels of success in the future. They strive to follow the procedures and implement the processes of the organization without truly understanding the context of the situation they are in and the impact on the relationships they have with others. There are two primary reasons for this: 1) the environments they operate in constantly change; and 2) individuals are given tasks or placed in jobs without understanding the importance of relationships in helping them be successful.

Not all scenarios are exactly the same, but there are a number of consistent drivers regardless of culture or industry. Here are some scenarios where individuals need the ability to build relationships:

Expanding globalization
Mergers and acquisitions
Organizational restructurings
Technology implementations
Process improvement initiatives
Strategic program launches
Diversity initiatives
Changing market forces
Changing government regulations and the need for compliance
More frequent job transitions, transfers, and turnover
The impact of changes by our competitors and how they go to market

These represent only a portion of the initiatives that drive change and the resulting conflict. These factors also change over time. The challenge is not to try to limit the changes, but to be out in front adapting and taking advantage of them. The key point is that there will always be change and we must be prepared to effectively deal with it—being proactive and making things happen rather than being reactive and having things happen to us.

When one looks at trade journals and publications, it is clear that organizations invest enormous amounts of money and make significant efforts to support employees in their work. One need only look within one's own organization to see the resources made available to training and developing its people. Yet, these processes and technologies—tools that are designed to give employees what they need to help them adapt to change—are not enough. Why not?

We started to ask that very question. We found it interesting that with all of the capacity and seemingly unlimited opportunity to improve and advance within an organization, so many people have such a difficult time dealing with the changes their organizations go through. People become frustrated, disillusioned, and demoralized. In a growing number of situations more people give up and go to look for opportunities elsewhere. As a side note, today it is common for individuals to change jobs every two to three years. The costs associated with this turnover and loss of talent go beyond the costs of hiring and training. It also includes the cost of missed opportunities by not having the right people, in the right roles, at the right time. The goal is to retain key talent in the organization.

There are many reasons people choose to leave a department, job, or organization. We have broken this down into what we call "push" and "pull" factors.

1. *Push* factors would be considered areas in the current environment that are not pleasant. Many of these reasons involve characteristics of the culture: poor work conditions, restrictions on social norms, and obstacles in getting the work done. Some examples include negative treatment by peers or supervisors, project work that does not let individuals utilize their current skills, and an environment that does not provide an opportunity for individuals to learn and develop new skills. Lack of rewards and recognition is also a major factor in pushing individuals out of an organization.
2. *Pull* factors, on the other hand, are seen as better opportunities outside the existing group, department, or organization. Such opportunities present themselves in ways that allow individuals to better position themselves for the future. Examples include internal departments or external organizations with good public reputations; companies that have a reputation for having

a good work environment, projects that let people utilize their current skills and provide an opportunity to develop new ones, more money, better rewards, and more opportunities for promotion and advancement. People are attracted by the environment and opportunities available.

To find out why people become dissatisfied, unproductive, and disengaged, we began to look at how people interact with each other on the job. We concluded that there are two key turning points that have a significant impact on performance: realizing our interpersonal interactions with others are not effective and feeling there is no way to change things to make the situation better.

1. <u>Realizing our interpersonal interactions with others in the organization are not effective</u>. Here a realization emerges that the hope and promise of achieving our goals and being successful do not seem like they can be accomplished due to the relationships we have with others in the organization. We find others do not have the same priorities, and we realize change is not likely to happen. This becomes emotionally draining, and frustration sets in. Individuals change their approach and attitude away from their work and the organization they are part of. They go from having energy and being motivated to being disillusioned and frustrated.
2. <u>Feeling there is no way to change things to make the situation better</u>. Here the feeling of being trapped sets in. That no matter what we do, nothing will change. It is not about the quality of our work, but the way the organization as a system works. We cannot figure out how to change our current situation so we decide to survive and look for opportunities elsewhere rather than putting our best effort into the current environment.

People build an organization. Supporting them helps foster an organization that will not only exist, it will accomplish goals more often and more effectively. It is important to understand that what has made us successful in the past may not help us identify things that can make us successful in the future, but that is only part of the problem.

The key is to learn how to read a situation, recognize what is going on with people-processes-change, and be able to adapt. Our goal in writing this book is to help you identify when you are in a situation that is not as effective as it can be and to look at ways to prevent interactions from having a negative impact on the overall goals of the organization, and the success of the individuals in it. The end result comes from working with others to create a culture that allows for open interactions between individuals, and enables them to do so within the ever-evolving organizational landscape.

This book takes a very direct approach, and asks you to take a look at your department, your coworkers, your managers, and yourself. But first, let's look at one key factor in successful organizations, trust.

A Matter of Risk and Trust

Take a few minutes to think about someone you trust and then look at the picture below.

TRUST TRIAD

When I have CONFIDENCE in someone...
Then I have less FEAR of consequences...
And I am willing to RISK more in the relationship.

Think about the three sides of the triangle. Would you agree that any of the following statements can apply in all dimensions of your life... personal, recreational, and professional?

- If I have confidence in those around me, I have less fear of consequences, and that allows me to try more things and take more risk.
- If I take more risk, I learn more, and therefore have less to fear. I become more confident in myself and the others with whom I interact.
- If I manage my fear, I am more open to taking on greater challenges. I can more effectively evaluate and accept risks that go with them. I become more confident and I learn and develop more quickly.

Now, think of all the individuals you come into contact with at work, whether you have contact with them on a day-to-day basis or more infrequently. Can you say that the above three dimensions of trust reflect your relationship with everyone on your team, in your department, or in your organization? If you are one of those who can honestly answer *yes* to this question, you are fortunate. For the rest of us, the situation is not as clear and there may be relationships that make you want to hold back on how much you share because you do not completely trust others. Let's further explore what we mean by these three key dimensions of trust—confidence, fear, risk.

Confidence

The term "confidence" can mean different things to people in different situations; we would like to suggest the following working definition:

> *Confidence is believing that you are able to handle a situation to obtain an acceptable outcome, being able to gain support and assistance if needed. When you are confident, you are likely to feel self-assured, self-reliant, and certain. More importantly your chances of being successful increase.*

Confidence in ourselves allows us to do what we do well. It also allows us to continue to grow and develop. If we are confident we can handle situations and issues that arise, we will take on more challenges, and try more things. It allows us to perform better.

Confidence in others allows us to count on them to do what they do well. It allows us to pursue our own work knowing that others will meet their goals, seek help or advice when needed, and pull their weight on the projects they are working on.

Confidence in the team allows all of us to work together to accomplish our goals with fewer stresses. We know we can rely on others and we can do our best to support them in return.

Confidence in the organization allows us to understand how our work is contributing to the bigger picture. We feel supported by the organization while being connected and working toward personal and organizational goals. We do the things we need to get the job done the best we can, even under difficult circumstances. We do not fear making a mistake.

> ### *Sidebar: Examples of how confidence is shown/developed.*
>
> Think of a great teacher or coach you had—grade school, high school, college—any one. Chances are you were encouraged to try, even if you got it wrong. You were encouraged to learn from what went wrong and to try again. It helped when you had a parent, teacher, coach, or peer encouraging you and providing feedback.
>
> Recall what it was like learning to ride a bike, drive a car, or play on a sports team. If you think about it, you did not just get on a bike and ride; it took time and practice. You learned by doing. If you were fortunate you had help from others who allowed you to conquer the challenge more quickly and in some cases with less pain.
>
> Learning a complex business process, technology system, or project is no different than learning any other complex task. Too often in adulthood individuals fear that showing they don't know something is a weakness and something that will be used against them—especially in front of peers or in a competitive culture. It makes building skills, and the confidence to use those skills, much more difficult. It makes seeking help a near impossibility. As a result, individuals and organizations are not as effective as they could be and it reflects back on performance.

Fear

Fear is one of those emotions that is not only necessary, but can be both good and bad. There are many ways fear is described, and being situation dependent, it can have many causes. For a working definition of fear in the context of a typical work environment, think about it this way:

> *Fear is having apprehension, anxiety, or trepidation about a situation or course of action. It often causes us to be more cautious or self-protective. When*

we are fearful. we are less likely to take chances, confront issues, or openly question the situation at hand or the people involved. Fear becomes the primary focus rather than accomplishing the goal or completing the task.

Personal fear can hold us back; we may tend to focus too much time and energy on negative consequences. We may do so because we have been hurt in the past or maybe it is due to things we have seen occur to others in our environment. If we are apprehensive about what can go wrong, that uncertainty can be enough to cause doubt and enable others to control and even manipulate us. Personal fear can lead to inaction when we are faced with a problem. We focus on what can go wrong rather than what can go right.

Fear of others or fear within the team can cause team members to focus too much on what might happen if things go wrong, if mistakes are made, or if team members disagree. Afraid of becoming scapegoats, some individuals may spend a substantial amount of time in self-protection activities, which adds to their stress at work. Some individuals undermine themselves by resorting to inaction when faced with a decision; they let others make decisions that may not be the best and they let others take credit for their work. They do not have control and often let things go in a direction they don't want.

Fear of the organization can have negative results. Fear of losing one's job, being passed over for promotions, or of losing one's reputation in the company can cause anxiety. When an organization "shoots the messenger," or is intolerant of mistakes, people become demoralized. They focus on tasks and not on results.

Unwilling or unable to trust that their careers are safe in an organization, individuals may choose to start over somewhere else. Even worse, they may stay, and become unproductive. They may not develop their full potential. They may also negatively impact their peers, or just complain about the environment and count the years to retirement.

- Highly visible—highly vulnerable individuals, who are in a succession pool or on a high-potential list, may fear losing those positions or opportunities. They may become cautious and reluctant to make a bold stand.
- Individuals may also have a fear of consequences and, therefore, become less likely to take initiative. These individuals may coast along, never having an impact on the organization or their careers. This can be worse than quitting or being fired. Also, because they underperform, they are not recognized for their ability and the organization never benefits from their efforts. The sad fact is that a number of individuals go through life like this.

Freedom from fear, on the other hand, can allow one to focus on doing the best job, with fewer stresses and less anxiety. Individuals enjoy their work more when they are not backing up all of their actions with documentation and justification to cover their actions in case something goes wrong. If we have an environment where we can learn from our mistakes, we grow personally, the team grows collectively, and the organization benefits as a whole. We can accomplish more and can more easily move our careers forward.

Risk

Risk, like fear, is situation dependent. Risk typically carries consequences, positive and negative, yet we most frequently focus on the negative aspects. We can be tempted to think of risk in relation to our jobs; in other words, the amount of risk we can take is often related to our role in an organization.

Think about the following description in relation to your own job.

Risk is exposing ourselves or our team to potential loss. In making any decision there is a tolerable level of risk, but this varies by individual and is based on how one sees the level of risk and the consequences or rewards associated with it. When we take risks, we generally accept that there may be uncertainty or threat. We also risk doing so well that more is expected of us than others and we become overburdened by demands and additional work.

Personal risk is making a decision that places us in a position of accountability. It allows us to grow as a person through our successes from the lessons we learn. It can also help us build confidence and overcome fears.

Team risk enables everyone to have a stake in the outcome. Spreading the decisions, actions, and consequences among the team members, enables us to work toward the shared goals of the team. It ensures that no single person is responsible for, or gets all the credit for, the collective work that the team accomplishes. No one person is to blame for failure.

Organizational risk helps ensure the company is successful. By developing new products and services, entering new markets, and improving processes, a company can create an environment where employees see their contributions and how they add value.

SIDEBAR...Three Keys to Building Personal Trust

In this book we show you how you can identify and manage the three components in reducing risk and building trust. We also look at many of the key barriers that get in the way. We will help you learn how to:

1) Understand and build personal confidence:
   - Understand how to see a situation for what it is, and how to evaluate alternatives:
     – how to read the situation; evaluate options, identify risks and rewards, and potential consequences.
     – how to understand yourself and how you will react in the situation.
   - Understand the impact of stress on our thinking, and how seeing ourselves as successful in a situation improves our odds for success.

2) Recognize and manage personal fear:
   - Accept fear as a normal reaction to a perceived threat. If you can identify the threat, you can plan around it. It allows you to identify options and the potential impact that a threat can have.
   - Identify where the fear is coming from—not the specific event, but the underlying drivers of uncertainty and doubt:
     – Evaluating the current situation.
     – Finding and solving the underlying problem, not just treating the symptoms.
   - Understand how fear is fed by the impact of perceived consequences from/on: work, family, success, security, and the "road-not-taken" perspectives.
   - Ask "What is the worst that can happen?"

3) Understand what is at risk and how to manage the risk, such as
   - Rewards that are at risk
   - Consequences of actions
   - Punishments as a result of action/inaction
   - Damages to self, career, future, etc.

Risking More...Getting More in Return

We have spent time linking three key concepts that, together, form a way to talk about trust—confidence, fear, risk. We decided to focus on these three key areas that help keep trust alive between people because trust depends on all three to some degree. While we would like to think we can trust those we work and associate with, we do so at different levels, for different reasons, and with different perceived consequences. We will go into greater detail about the types of barriers and obstacles that impact us and how we hold back trust. But before we do, let's look at what builds trust and what destroys trust.

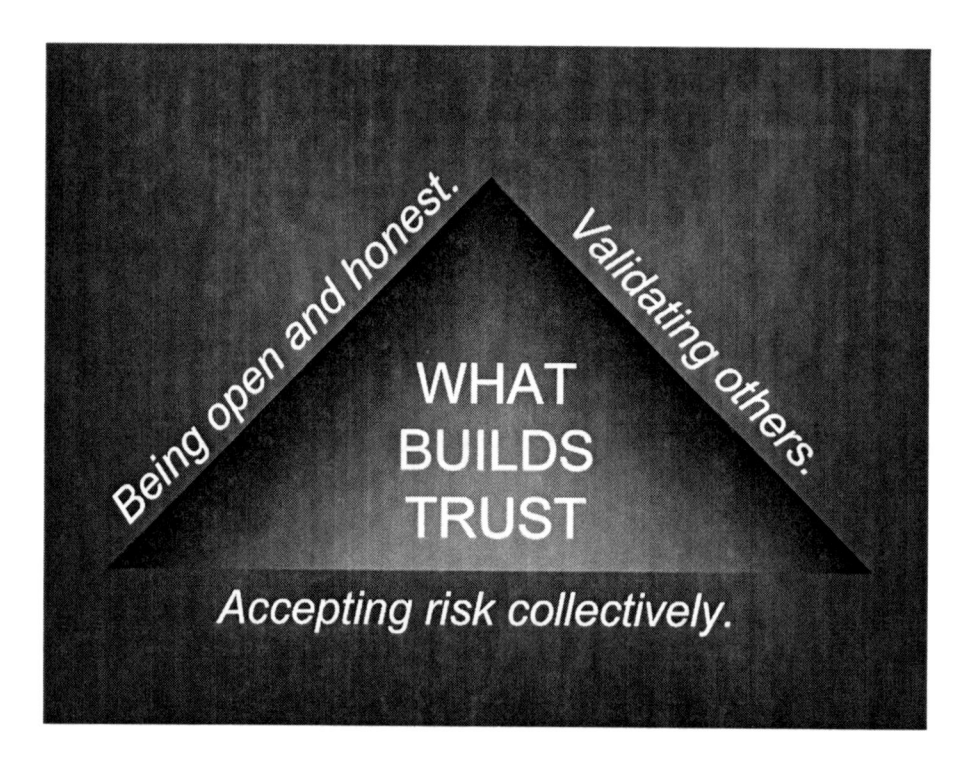

What Builds Trust

WHAT BUILDS TRUST

- Being open and honest.
- Validating others.
- *Accepting risk collectively.*

To build trust, one has to take risks.

- We have to risk being open and honest in the right way so that others can be open and honest with us in return. While it seems obvious on the surface, it is hard to do.
- We also have to validate others so we let them know we are not afraid to let them shine in their own spotlight.
- Finally, we have to accept responsibility for the risk we are personally taking in individual and group interactions. Let's look at these a little closer.

Being Open and Honest

The first key to building trust is to be open and honest in our interactions with others. By this we mean, telling the truth and not leaving out facts that would impact how someone would judge a situation. Look at the following statements; you probably have experienced at least one. Think of the importance of communication and the need to be clear, accurate, open, and honest.

- Have you ever held back on the amount of information you presented? Presenting a fact at a time and waiting to see what the response was before presenting any more. If you presented more was it what you originally intended? Was what you ended up presenting accurate for the situation at hand?
- Have you ever been in a conversation where it was obvious the other person was listening to "respond" rather than listening to "understand"? Did you change or modify what you wanted to say because of it?
- Are your actions in line with your words and your promises? Do you walk the talk?
- Do you act with integrity, making sure your words and actions are in line with the situation at hand? Can others take risks based on your word?

Validating Others

The second key to building trust involves the way in which we interact with others. It is important in our interactions with others to make the effort to treat them fairly.

- Do you share the credit and truthfully acknowledge others' efforts in the work?
- Do you guide and assist others in accomplishing their goals?
- Do you support others and provide positive, accurate feedback to help them improve?
- Do you build confidence in others through your words and actions?
- Do you focus on successes and lessons learned, rather than failures that can cause others to feel rejected, disappointed, or demoralized?

Accepting Risk Collectively

The third key to building trust centers on the personal risk we take in a relationship. When we interact with others, there is always the potential for the relationship to change. We take that risk every time we associate with someone. We need to be mindful that our actions and words can have any number of effects on others, even though the other people may not respond to what we are saying or doing, we impact them. When things go wrong...

- Do you take responsibility or seek to blame others?
- Do you protect others from situations that have the potential to result in failure?
- Do you not only hold the appropriate parties accountable, do you also help them understand their mistakes?
- Do you provide valid and useful feedback and are you open to hearing the feedback others have for you?

> ***Put into Practice***
>
> The questions in these three categories can be used as the basis for team building. Asking these questions in a facilitated session can help the team improve its effectiveness and build a base for relationships to improve and grow.

What Destroys Trust

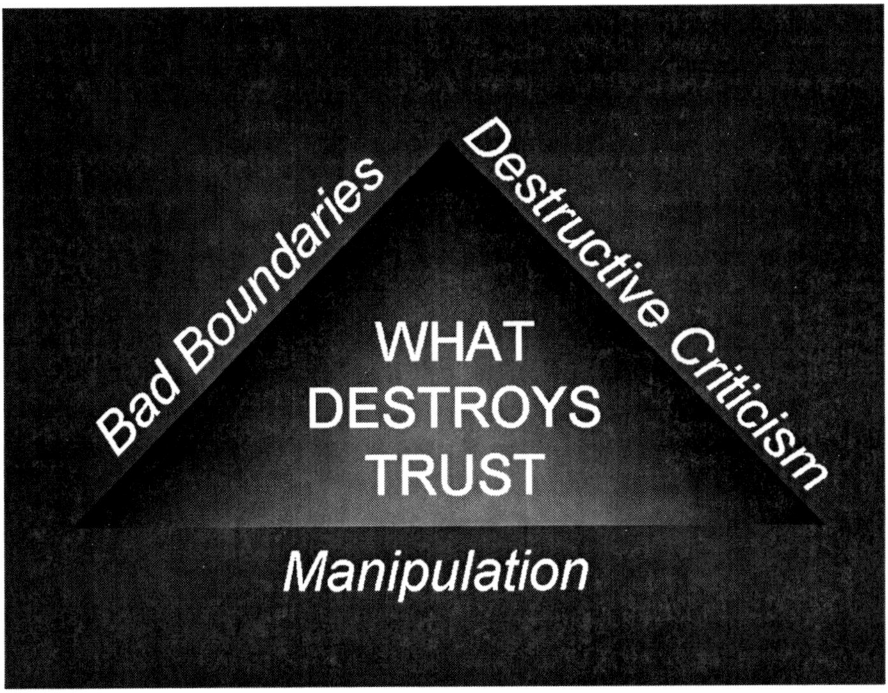
Bad Boundaries
Destructive Criticism
WHAT DESTROYS TRUST
Manipulation

Trust is destroyed when a person, group, or organization *consciously* or *deliberately* hurts an individual—it is often seen as betrayal. However, it is also very important to keep in mind that people have different perspectives on what trust is and when it is broken. While many people can forgive a mistake or a broken promise, when it becomes a repeated pattern of action, or when the other person is injured by deliberate action, it becomes harder to view the other person as something other than self-serving, malicious, or mean. Some individuals may not trust another person until they get to know them. On the other hand, others may trust people initially until they are hurt by them in some way. Regardless, trust is destroyed when we see the negative actions against us as *deliberate* on the part of the other person.

Bad Boundaries

A primary factor that leads to the destruction of trust is having "bad boundaries." In others words, when an individual does not respect the personal rights, opinions, and actions of others a relationship deteriorates. Bad boundaries come into play when a person ignores where their space ends and the other person's space begins. They might impose themselves on others when they are neither needed nor wanted. They might try to control the situation as well as the people involved. They impose their beliefs, values, and ways of doing things on others. They may even manipulate others in order to get what they want. Here are a few ways individuals are seen as having created bad boundaries and taking advantage of others.

- Pawning their work off on others.
- Taking credit for the team's effort and results.
- Raising standards for others until they are too high. *There is a natural limit to how much something can be improved, or how short a deadline can be made.*
- Imposing on others' time and work.
- Controlling what is not in their area of responsibility.

Destructive Criticism

The second factor in destroying trust involves criticizing others. Here we are talking about pointing out an individuals mistakes without regard for how that criticism will impact them, their feelings, and their subsequent performance. Think of this as the opposite of the trust-building skill of being open and honest in order to help an individual grow and develop.

If your goal is to provide feedback, it needs to be done in a way that makes others aware of the mistake, situation, or error, while at the same time not making them feel negative about themselves or their work. By providing a clear and accurate assessment of what occurred, what improvement is needed, and what you can do to help them improve, you open the door to a much stronger relationship. Think about the following ways in which people are seen as being destructive in their criticism of others.

- Putting someone down to make himself or herself look better.
- Misrepresenting someone's work to deflate them (e.g., not telling them they did a good job, but telling them they have to do better).
- Accusatory language. "If you had done that...then this wouldn't have happened."
- Speaking poorly of others' work, gossiping, downplaying the importance of a team member's contribution.

Manipulation

The third factor in destroying trust is manipulation. Unfortunately, it can be done so subtly that it is often not recognized until after the relationship is damaged. Think of manipulation as being the key factor that causes us to withdraw from certain individuals, to avoid taking any risk in the relationships we have with them, and to spend a lot of time and effort proving ourselves. Think about the following ways that people have manipulated others. We would bet you have seen these on more than one occasion.

- Withholding information.
- Lies, misdirection, selective application of facts.
- Misrepresentation of a situation.
- Avoiding responsibility.
- Hiding motives.
- Insincere flattery to get one's own way.

- Direct or implied threats.
- Promise of rewards or threats of punishment.

Activity and Worksheet

Unfortunately, it is often difficult to see a situation for what it is when we are in the middle of it. Worse, even if we understand it, we may not know what to do about it. One thing is certain, it is almost impossible to solve a problem or handle a situation we don't understand. The following activity will help you think through a difficult situation so that you can put some of what you read to a useful purpose.

Step 1. Think about a difficult situation or a problem that you could have handled better. It should be something that, after it was all over and done, you discovered there was a better way you could have handled it. For example, maybe you tried to help someone by giving them feedback on their performance, but rather than seeing your feedback as helpful she became offended and filed a grievance against you. At the time, there was no indication she was upset. Another possible example would be where you told a peer there was an issue with his report. It was at the end of the day and you didn't take the time to explain what was wrong because you were in a hurry to leave. Over the course of the next several weeks, your peer avoided you so you went to him to find out why. He told you he was offended that you said the report was wrong and you didn't take the time to talk to him about why.

Step 2. Using the worksheet that follows, answer the questions the best as you can. Remember that there are no right or wrong answers, and no one has to see this but you.

Worksheet – Think of a situation you were involved in that did not go well.

1. What could you have handled better?

2. In hindsight, what led up to the situation?

3. What were things you see now, that you didn't see then?

4. What were the relationships between the people involved? What did each have at stake?

5. What was the sequence of events that played out, step-by-step (at a high level)?

6. What were your reactions?

7. What were your anxieties and worries?

8. What were the contributing fears?

9. What types of stress were influencing you at the time?

10. What was at risk?

11. What were the barriers you faced?

12. How did the type of relationship you had with the person impact the situation?

13. In retrospect, did you learn anything that you could have done better?

14. What have you done since then to become better at handling such situations?

If you look at more than one situation, do you see a recurring pattern of issues? You can also use the preceding worksheet to help you work through and analyze relationships you are having difficulty with and compare them to successful ones.

What's Next

Think about people you were associated with during a time when there was a lot at risk. Maybe it was taking on a new job, switching to a different department or hiring a new team member. Then think about the following statement and see if you can agree with it:

If we are open and honest with one another, then we can validate one another as people and through our interactions; together we can accept and manage the risks associated with the endeavor. We don't fear what we don't know because we trust others not to take advantage of us.

Now, think about what really took place during that time. Confidence, fear, risk, and trust, probably all played into your decision making process. If you are like us, you probably had good and bad things happen. But, when the bad things happened, you told yourself, "That sure taught me a lesson. I'll never do that again." If things went well, it reinforced your approach and how you handled similar situations that followed. If things did not go well, you either changed your approach or tried to avoid situations like that altogether. Ask yourself if any of those experiences put a shadow over you and some of your subsequent decisions, choices, and interactions.

- Maybe you learned not to sign off on anything until you read it and had someone else read it to make sure there were no issues.
- Maybe you learned not to trust a particular person in management.
- Maybe you learned you have to put everything in writing all the time.

Whatever you learned, you are not alone. Consider this, all of those lessons you learned over the years are impacting not only you, but everyone else around you. *What you see is a lot of people, doing lots of things that show they do not really trust one another. They are simply trying to protect themselves.*

When this happens, or is taken to extremes, such behaviors become what we are calling *intrinsic cultural barriers* to performance and trust.

> *Intrinsic*, because they become ingrained in the individual, team, department, and even the organization's practices. They occur regularly and are the standard way individuals are expected to deal with situations.
>
> *Cultural*, because they become social norms—the unspoken behaviors people learn to live by. They are accepted as *"the way things are done around here,"* or the *"status quo."* People learn to live with them. They often don't question them.
>
> *Barriers*, because they stop individuals from doing their best. They interfere with teamwork, performance, and progress.

It is our belief that if you can identify the barriers, recognize yourself in the situation and determine what is causing you fear or worry, you will be able to manage the risk and increase your level of success and satisfaction in life and effectiveness on the job. Our goal is to help show you ways to understand and overcome some of the barriers that hold you back from being truly successful.

Key Points:

- "Push factors" are negative aspects in the current environment that cause people to want to leave. "Pull factors" are seen as positive aspects in other environments that cause people to want to be part of that other environment rather than the one they are currently part of.

- The three dimensions of trust are; confidence, fear, and risk. The more confidence people have in others, the less they fear them doing something wrong, which opens the relationship to grow, because risk is seen as being less of a factor.

- Trust is built in relationships by being open and honest, by validating others, and by accepting risk collectively.

- Trust is destroyed in relationships when the respect of others is violated (bad boundaries), when criticism is destructive (focused on the individual and not the issues), and when manipulation not cooperation is the method used to get things done.

CHAPTER 2.
COMMON BARRIERS TO BUILDING TRUST

Chapter Goals:

- Be able to identify "enablers" and "inhibitors" to building trust.

- Understand three key solution techniques to help in building trust.

- See how barriers are built and what can be done to overcome them.

- Differentiate between "getting results" and getting results the "right way".

- Understand how actions impact individuals, teams, and organizations.

Where it All Begins

Our ability to trust others and our capacity to accept risk are based on factors that include:

- Our past experiences in relationships—personal, casual, and professional.
  – Recall your favorite boss, teacher, coworker, or friend. Ask yourself why you remember him or her. It is most likely something the person did for you that made you feel good about yourself or showed that he or she really cared about you.

- Expectations of a relationship include the things we need and want from the other person and what we feel we can offer in return. An important factor in a successful relationship is whether our individual goals are compatible with those of others and the organization we are part of.
  - Consider whether your focus is long or short term. Ask yourself whether you would accept a position with a company if you had information it was relocating to another state within the coming year. Would you focus on the immediate opportunity or would you look at the longer-term opportunity? How would this impact the types of relationships you would build with others in this particular organization? Often we judge the relationship based on our expectations without regard for the fact the relationship can outlast the circumstances under which the relationship was formed. Do you build relationships around the job, or do you build relationships based on the commonalities and professional interests you have with the individuals you interact with?
  - Are there any organizations you would not want to work for under any circumstances? Is it because of their reputation? The products or services they produce? The people who work there? Having personal values that are compatible with organizational values increases the likelihood of success an individual will have in an organization.
  - What do you do when your personal needs and goals are not met in the relationship, or are in conflict with the other individuals or group? Do you address them with the person directly or wait and see what happens over a period of time? Do you deal with the differences or try to avoid them?
- Expectations related to how long you expect the relationship will last, and what the purpose of the relationship is.
  - Ask yourself whether the fact that your relationship is short-term or long-term affects how you handle your interactions. For example, think about how you might interact

with a supervisor, professor, or coworker, as compared to a spouse, your parent, or your child.

How we handle the factors that influence relationships on an individual, team, and organizational level impacts the type of barriers we build between ourselves and others. Before we discuss the barriers individually, let's look at some factors that enable and inhibit our ability to build trust. Ask yourself what is it that "enables" *you* to build trust with *others*. Some of the more common enablers include:

- The level of comfort you have with someone.
- The degree to which you have common goals and beliefs.
- The shared experiences you have had with others. These may include those with whom you have had similar life experiences, such as similar upbringing, same type of schooling, participation in similar sports or other common social activities.

It is also important to understand what "inhibits" you from building trust with others. Some of the more common inhibitors include:

- Lack of agreement on goals and processes.
- Different biases related to individuals and organizations.
- Different priorities in what and how things should be done.

A starting point to enable a greater level of trust begins with understanding what others are trying to accomplish and why. You may not agree on goals and priorities, but by understanding what each party is trying to accomplish you create a greater level of respect for each other. Look for common areas of agreement and build on them. When there are areas of disagreement, try to understand why. Is the disagreement based on the overall goal, the process, or the specific interests of the parties involved?

An example would be to ask a group, "Should the problem of world hunger be solved?" You will most likely get strong agreement that it should, but if you ask, "How should we solve world hunger?" You will most likely get a number of different responses on how to accomplish it.

Look to see where goals and priorities overlap. Are there any areas that, by working together, both parties will benefit? Finding any type of common ground is key to developing a better relationship. By focusing on things we have in common it gives us time to understand and learn about each other. It provides the opportunity to ask questions and explore how others think, make decisions, and communicate.

Another helpful tool is to try to put yourself in the other person's place and see how it may change your responses and feelings. Sometimes there are underlying factors that impact how we see the world and how we make decisions. Long-held beliefs can take time to change.

WORKSHEET: Things that "Enable" or "Inhibit" Trust

Using the table below, take a few minutes to consider a recent relationship issue that was problematic for you. What were some of the factors that enabled and inhibited you as you tried to work through the issues and challenges? By using this technique, you can better understand the issues from a more objective point of view so you can work through them more effectively.

ENABLERS	INHIBITORS

Enablers provide strengths to build on and are often the easiest area to focus on. Inhibitors often result from simple misunderstandings. The starting point is to listen to the other side and make sure each party knows why the others believe the way they do. While it is often easier to let first impressions guide our attitudes toward others, we need to be careful not to prejudge.

In our work we frequently have client groups participate on advisory panels related to the projects we are working on. We do this so they understand and learn what we do and why. We involve them for a number of reasons. First, is to get their input into identifying the problem or opportunity. We want them to feel they are heard. Second, is that by getting their input they are part of building the solution and as a result we get buy in along the way. Clients typically like being involved in creating something or resolving an issue. An additional benefit is that by having up-to-date insights on what is happening with our work they can more effectively plan and integrate the changes into their work and manage how it directly impacts them.

There are three key techniques that help foster collaboration and trust:
- Engage people in the situation. Keep them informed of what is happening, especially when they will be impacted by the outcome. Ensure everyone is aware of the overall goal and their role in making it happen—communicate.
- Invite dialog and invite participation. Involve people; don't shut them out of the process. Ask questions; listen to what they have to say. Give credit, thank individuals for their input.
- Accept whatever happens without placing blame. Even if there are negative outcomes, support the team's efforts. The focus should be on addressing the issue not blaming an individual. Learn from mistakes, but do not relive or repeat them. Learn from experience.

3 Key Solution Techniques

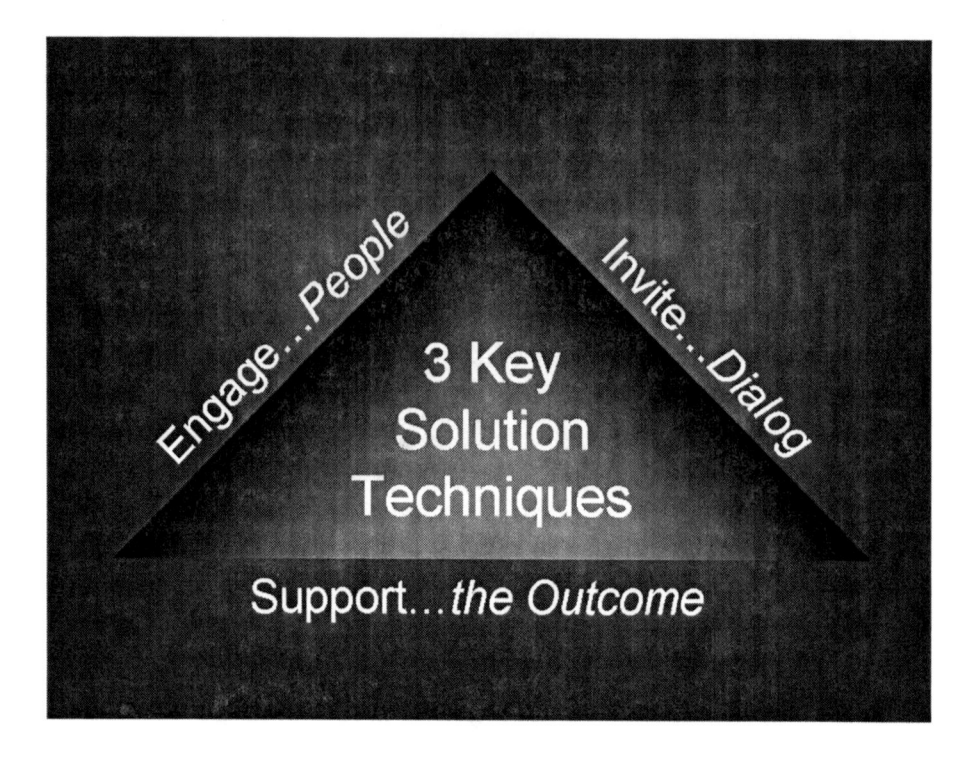

Engage...People
Invite...Dialog
Support...*the Outcome*

Actions that Build Barriers

Barriers between people can happen almost immediately. A small gesture or symbol can send the wrong message and get a relationship off to a bad start. You often see this with stereotypes of different groups, genders, religions, and people with differing political perspectives.

Consider the example of a man who is an accountant. He is also a dedicated member of the Republican Political Party. Originally he works for a defense contractor where the majority of individuals and coworkers are also Republicans. He organizes political rallies and fund-raisers and his supervisor even gives him time off to support these activities. Then the market changes, his job is eliminated, and he finds a new job opportunity with a financial services organization. He soon finds that his new organization frowns upon politics and political activities in the workplace. When he puts up pictures of himself with well-known Republican Party officials he also discovers that most of his coworkers are members of the Democratic Party. His new coworkers now avoid and isolate him. This has nothing to do with his work or skills, but is simply because of his political beliefs. He soon becomes frustrated and leaves the organization.

Barriers can compound over time from many different causes. Once they start to build, they not only impact individual interactions but can become entrenched in the culture of an organization. They manifest themselves in very distinct patterns of behavior. These patterns, when allowed to take hold, become accepted behavior. People begin to accept things as they are because it is easier than trying to change them, whether they are for better or worse. The issue is the effort and risk involved in changing, and not whether changing is the right thing to do. In the long run, the common causes of mistrust create environments where people don't like to work or socialize. They complain, but don't do anything about it. The overall impact on morale is negative and unless things are changed performance suffers.

Here are a few common barriers to building trust. We will discuss how these acts combine to create poisonous cultures where people, productivity, and performance are impacted. You will see how these obvious acts can go undetected and unnoticed when they occur within the context of work and social situations.

Seeking to Find Fault or Reprimand

During the normal course of work, problems occur and mistakes are made. In the process of trying to identify the cause of a problem, individuals often try to identify who made the mistake rather than why the mistake was made. By focusing on blaming individuals rather than learning from the mistake that was made, relationships are strained rather than strengthened. Think about it this way—no one likes to feel under attack. If we build on what we learn, rather than look to blame others, our relationships and level of trust become stronger and our relationships grow.

Breaking Confidences

The importance of creating a culture of openness cannot be overstated. Individuals need to know that what they say and do won't come back to haunt them. Consider the example of an employee sharing personal information with his or her boss so the two of them may be more effective in resolving a problem that exists with a client. Think about how the employee would feel if the information that was shared in confidence shows up as a "weakness" on his or her performance review six months later. In addition to having feelings of hurt, anger, and betrayal, there may also be tangible consequences such as a lost promotion or pay raise. Individuals need to be confident that what they tell others will not come back and be used against them.

Disclosing and Twisting Information

Often individuals tell others something in confidence or "off the record" and are then surprised when what they said is known by everyone in the organization. Even worse is when the accuracy of the story is incorrect or when others have changed what you said. The best policy is to remember nothing is ever "off the record." Another challenge is when others only hear part of a conversation and "fill in the rest" with what they think will make an interesting story. If it's important or there is a possibility of misinterpretation consider putting it in writing.

Individuals need to know that others won't use information they overhear against them. Consider, for a moment, the case where a supervisor overheard a conversation in which an employee was on the phone with an attorney about new legislation that would impact the department if it passed. Imagine the individual's surprise and embarrassment when the supervisor came to him telling him if he was having legal problems they should not interfere with the quality of his work. The issue was not that the individual was having legal problems; in reality, he was having a conversation with an attorney related to a work project. The point is that there is now a perception in the workplace that the individual has legal problems. This is something that could be tough to overcome. No matter how you handle it, there will be consequences. The issue is that once your reputation is damaged, regardless of whether it is justified or not, it is difficult to overcome.

When managers look for someone for a key assignment, they look for people who will not be sidetracked or controversial. Hearing rumors like we mentioned here, whether substantiated or not, impacts a person's reputation and how others perceive him or her. The person may be seen as a risk. The focus is shifted from what a person is capable of doing on the job to what may be seen as detractors from getting the job done. If things go wrong, the manager's decision making may be questioned. Most managers will not take the risk. Think of it like this...

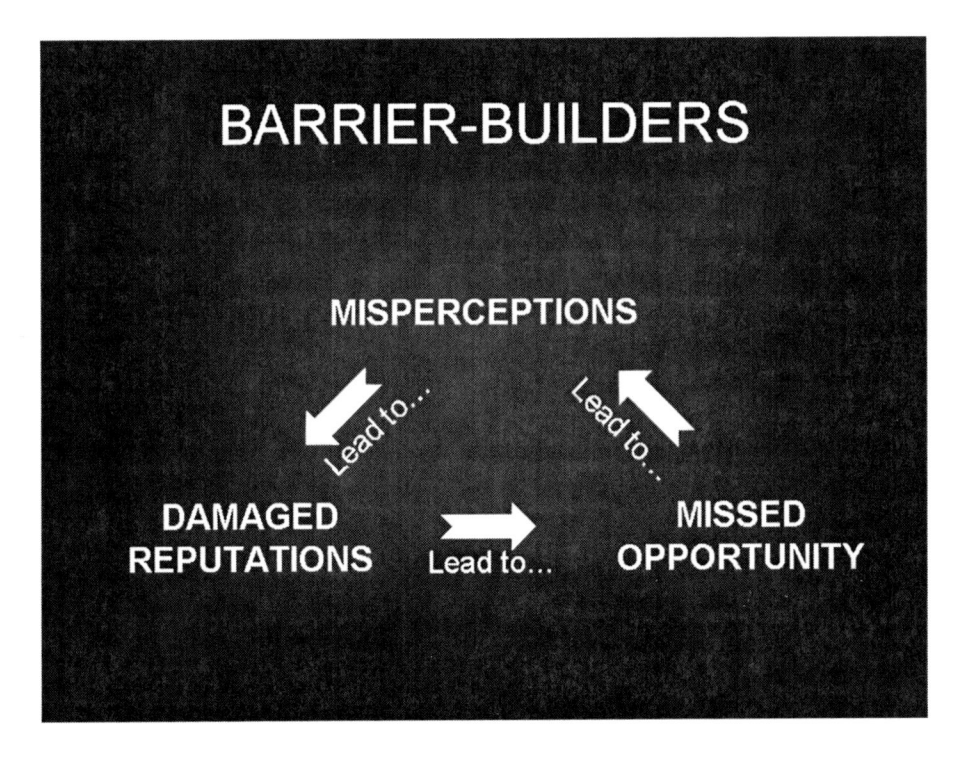

BARRIER-BUILDERS

MISPERCEPTIONS *Lead to...* DAMAGED REPUTATIONS *Lead to...* MISSED OPPORTUNITY

It is also important not to be caught off guard by trick questions. "No comment" is not a good response when asked a question such as "Do you still have a drinking problem?" Neither is "yes" or "no". Learn to turn the tables. A more appropriate response would be to calmly respond "I have never had a drinking problem. Why would you even make a statement like that?" You have now turned the tables and the questioner is the one left with a question to answer.

A culture where communication is open and feedback is honest (not necessarily all good or bad) allows any misperceptions to be addressed *before* individuals are judged, passed over, or written off. Reputations are not damaged. Individuals are free to pursue the best opportunities available without prejudice.

One needs only to look at the number of employment related lawsuits to see how costly misperceptions can be. Even more important are the destroyed careers and ruined lives that have occurred based on simple misperceptions.

Challenging Individuals in a Negative Way

Think about a time when someone challenged you in a hurtful, negative, or discouraging way. How did that affect your motivation, desire, or need to do a good job? In talking to people about their performance, there are always two important components to address:

1) What was accomplished.
2) How it was accomplished.

Individuals need feedback on both. The right results with unscrupulous methods of getting them can be more dangerous to an organization than having a person not achieve the results at all.

Right Results	Culture of "Winner Take All" No Collaboration	Successful Individual Successful Organization Collaboration, Sharing, Development
Wrong Results	Review Strategy Review Individual	Opportunity to Develop Organization and Individual Mentoring and Learning
	Wrong Way	Right Way

When we spend our time focusing on what is possibly wrong instead of what went well, we stifle innovation, hurt morale, and make people feel bad about the relationship. Individuals who work in an environment like this soon lose motivation. Team members who work with peers who do this can become unhappy and disengage from them. Friends who do this to others eventually go their separate ways.

Take for example when a new person comes into an organization. He or she usually comes in with energy, drive, and enthusiasm. Often within a short period of time the person loses that energy, drive and enthusiasm. Why? Because the person is ignored, criticized, or harassed. The person frequently hears "That's not how we do it here." The end result is a withdrawn, unmotivated individual, who may leave the organization within a fairly short period.

What happens in negative environments is that an individual's mindset switches from "What can I accomplish?" to "What can I do so I don't get punished?" Thinking shifts from "possibilities" to "consequences."

Motivating by Disapproval

Imagine you are ten years old and you bring home your report card, all A's and B's and one C. Instead of hearing "good job," you are told, "You need to work harder on bringing up that C." Such things occur in the workplace, in social situations, and in family situations. Some individuals get into the habit of never praising or rewarding, believing that this is the way to challenge and motivate individuals. Some individuals are motivated by such actions, but this type of motivation is limiting and does not encourage individuals to be creative. It is also important to point out that there are others who will be demotivated, discouraged, and may even give up before getting started.

Challenging people through negativity creates a culture where individuals hope the passing of time will change things. Those individuals do not perform to their potential and will wait and see if they can influence any change with the hope that the new manager and the new environment will be better than the last. This becomes a vicious cycle of ineffectiveness and lack of performance.

In order for individuals to perform well, they need feedback on what they are doing as well as on how they are doing it. To say "good job," doesn't say enough. Most individuals know, or at least hope, they are doing a good job. They may even assume they are doing a good job because they have not been told they need improvement or have not been fired. Providing specific feedback on what you want them to improve on, as well as on what they do well, allows individuals to understand what is expected of them.

How Barriers Are Built

The barriers to trust, and ultimately performance, that we are talking about in this chapter are incidents and situations that have the potential, if not addressed, to escalate until they become entrenched in the organization. As they become commonplace and expected or accepted by employees, they can be considered "intrinsic" to the culture. While they are generally noticed by individuals, they are often ignored and allowed to continue, or worse, escalate and compound.

Because these barriers evolve over time, they can build a toxic environment in the workplace. When allowed to continue, these barriers can even become ritualized, turning into social norms in and of themselves. Once accepted, you can hear employees making statements such as, "I work in a toxic department," or "My boss is bad, but what can I do about it?" You may hear managers saying, "This is what the culture is like. That is how it is, either adapt or leave." Guess what eventually happens—people leave. Or worse, they stay and negatively impact everyone around them.

If you think about it, a "culture" is made up of individuals. So, the issue is not just the culture, but the inability, unwillingness, or complacency of the people within the culture to confront a situation and do what is right.

Barriers impact one's ability to do the right thing. They add layers of unneeded and counterproductive control. They increase the effort needed to do the job and add to the burden on the employees at all levels in order to handle ineffective situations. While we know there are barriers, it helps to specifically point out what those barriers are and why they exist. Knowing what the problem is allows us to start to improve, if we choose to do so.

The following table lists common types of situations where barriers arise. If allowed to continue, they can have a negative impact on how individuals work together. Some individuals go along with the situation, only doing the minimum to keep them employed. Some quit. Some retaliate (unfortunate, but not unheard of). Some become passive or complacent. Others just stand by and watch. Here is a list of common barriers.

HOW BARRIERS AFFECT INDIVDUALS, TEAMS, AND ORGANIZATIONS

AS INDIVIDUALS, WE IMPACT OTHERS

Barrier	Description
Barrier #1: Misidentifying the Cause of the Problem and Solving the Symptoms. IMPACTS YOUR PERSONAL ABILITY TO RECOGNIZE AND SOLVE PROBLEMS	Misidentifying the cause of a problem occurs when a symptom is identified and one jumps to fix the symptom. The core of the problem is neither sought nor identified. Some action is taken to alleviate a problem temporarily, but a permanent fix is never identified or implemented. The consequence is that a situation occurs but one tries to stop it without first identifying what is going on. The problem comes up again, and if unsolved it leads to a cycle of treating symptoms. The real problem is never solved.

Barrier #2: Using Filters and Bias in Our Interactions. IMPACTS OUR ABILITY TO UNDERSTAND ANOTHER INDIVIDUAL'S POINT OF VIEW	When it comes to our own personal filters, they can alter the way we see things. Our filters are developed from many sources. Some come from our environment—what we have learned growing up in our families, and experiences we have had in our organizations. Our experiences impact how we create our own filters, whether positive or negative, and those experiences impact how we deal with new situations.
Barrier #3: Impact of Handoffs, Denial, and Delegation. IMPACTS YOUR PERSONAL REPUTATION AND ABILITY TO BUILD RELATIONSHIPS	There are many ways of defining and interpreting what a handoff represents, to both the person doing the handing off, as well as to the person receiving the handoff. In a positive situation, a handoff would be one way of helping a person develop new skills and talents, as well as learn more about the organization, its business, and its industry. However, when handoffs occur in such a way that there is negative intent or consequences; they can create a strong barrier to building relationships and accomplishing goals.

WE IMPACT OUR TEAMS...

Barrier #4: Diluting the Talent Base. IMPACTS TEAM STAFFING AND PERFORMANCE	Staffing a department, team, or project often requires that a compromise be made between desired outcomes and hiring the best talent to help achieve those outcomes. Sometimes, individuals who are hired or assigned to the various job functions or projects do not have the necessary experience or skills to do the work properly. Barriers occur when people are hired or replaced for reasons based on something other than talent and experience. Here are some interesting questions you may have pondered in the past: • Why is it that the most qualified people are often not hired or given the best opportunities? • What are some of the reasons people have been hired? • How is this going to impact my ability to get the job done?
Barrier #5: Avoiding Issues, Being Insensitive to Others' Needs, Interests, and Goals. IMPACTS TEAM COHESIVENESS AND HURTS PERSONAL RELATIONSHIPS	A barrier to trust occurs when an individual does not handle a problem or a situation that is brought to his or her attention, but instead does things purposely to avoid it. Worse, the individual may be told to handle it on his or her own or to minimize the issue. Regardless of who brought up the issue, it is still a problem that needs to be addressed.

Barrier #6: Controlling Behaviors—Disempowering at a Personal and Interpersonal Level. Controlling and Status Seeking at Someone Else's Expense. IMPACTS TEAM DYNAMICS	An individual's preferred style of working impacts the people, teams, and organizations they work with. One way to look at an individual's likelihood of success in an environment is based on the dimensions of "control" and "knowledge of the function" they are responsible for. This model can be applied to any job role, as it reflects a working style as opposed to a management style. Failure to understand and acknowledge others' working styles leads to a lack of commitment, and in some cases can even lead to sabotage of a project.

THERE ARE ORGANIZATIONAL IMPACTS

Barrier #7: Being Locked into the Status Quo, Focusing on Rituals Rather than Getting the Job Done. IMPACTS THE ORGANIZATION'S BENCH STRENGTH, COMPETITIVENESS AND LEVEL OF INNOVATION	An organization's culture is driven by a number of factors including how people relate to each other, how they communicate with each other, and how decisions are made. Often it is the "rules" of the culture and how they are followed that is more important than the work itself. Being aware of these factors can help you be more effective in successfully navigating through the organization.
Barrier #8: Allowing an Atmosphere of Mistrust. IMPACTS OVERALL EFFECTIVENESS	The cultural atmosphere can cause people to work together for good or ill will. People will build relationships based on how they perceive the motivations of others, and how they see them interacting with others. This, in turn, is a reflection of the prevailing attitudes toward trust.

WHAT CAN YOU DO?

Become people based. Build relationships that are open and honest.	Focusing on individuals, even when you are under time constraints, will positively impact team effectiveness.
	
	• It will build your personal reputation as someone who can be trusted. It will show the team you are open to the "how" to get it done, not just the demand to get it done.
	• It will bring more commitment to help achieve the goals.
	• It will help you develop better team work, resulting in improved:
	  − Team staffing
	  − Team cohesiveness
	  − Team dynamics
	  − Team performance
	  − Team innovation
	• It will help build a culture that is:
	  − Innovative
	  − One that attracts talented individuals; one that people want to be part of
	  − One that leverages people to gain a competitive advantage

Key Points:

- Enablers help us find ways to get things done. Inhibitors hold us back. Understanding what they are helps us build a strategy to build effective relationships.

- Engaging people, inviting dialog, and supporting outcomes are three solution techniques that help build trust.

- Barriers are built through misperceptions, which lead to damaged reputations, resulting in missed opportunities.

- It's not just getting results, but getting the right results in the right way that encourages teamwork and builds trust.

- Barriers hold back individuals, teams, and organizations from being as effective as possible. Understanding what they are and why they exist is the first step in overcoming them.

CHAPTER 3.
WHY FIXING SYMPTOMS DOSEN'T SOLVE PROBLEMS

Chapter Goals:

- Identify the types of problems we face in building relationships.

- Understand why fixing symptoms is easier than solving problems.

- Evaluate the impact on others by not addressing the real problem.

A Problem by Any Other Name...

To keep it simple, we will divide problems into three groups for your consideration.

- The first group contains the normal, everyday problems we all encounter in the course of doing business. Examples include broken machines, delayed deliveries, people out sick, deadline changes, reallocated resources, and so on. These are the typical events you encounter on a routine basis that you expect to deal with and solve during the normal course of business.
- The second group contains very serious problems that are unexpected and damaging. Examples include major accidents, destructive natural events, a major lawsuit or protest, and other problems that cause a major interruption in our work. These are major concerns that a business has to deal with, ones that lack precedent or history to help people work through them. These require everyone

to pull together and make sacrifices. One does not expect to solve these problems during the normal course of business, but instead expects to recover with as little loss as possible.
- The third group is the most detrimental to an organization's culture. It is where problems begin as small issues and quickly escalate as people either seek to avoid the issue in hopes it will resolve itself, or they seek to resolve it in their own best interests rather than seeking the optimal solution for all involved. Blaming others, covering up problems, and altering data and facts are common in these situations. The difference is that successful organizations deal with these issues effectively and move on. In other organizations such problems can affect employee performance, morale, productivity, and turnover. It can get to a point where the organization can no longer function. Problems in this area are categorized as artificial, contrived, and derived from situations that are outside of the normal business routine.

Often, people are in a position where they can exert authority or influence over individuals, projects, goals, and resources, but they do so selfishly so their personal goals are met at the expense of others.

Problems occur when a symptom is identified and one rushes to fix the symptom. The core of the problem is neither sought nor identified. Some action is taken to alleviate a problem temporarily, but a permanent fix is never identified or implemented. Some reasons this happens:

- Individuals fear they will be held responsible for the problem.
- There may be negative consequences for bringing a problem into the open.
- Being associated with a failed process, misguided product, or ineffective service may have a negative impact on an individual's career.

The consequence is that a vicious cycle of solutions gets applied to a problem that has not been fully identified. Time goes by, resources are wasted, and people become frustrated.

For example, consider a supervisor who has repeated production deficiencies and continually changes the *process* instead of analyzing the situation first to find out what is going on. For such a seemingly simple issue, consider the following, which we have seen a number of times in our own experiences:

- If the problem is not a broken process, changing the process only enables you to keep having a problem, but in a different way.
  - Taking the time to perform a root cause analysis will identify the problem because it forces you to ask "why" until the underlying cause of the problem is identified.
- Employees will make more mistakes and make them faster, taking a "shot-gun" approach.
  - If you have made assumptions and have not done any fact-finding, individuals will guess at what should be done and hope that it will work.
- Employees will experience the exasperating "domino effect."
  - Changing one thing may result in "unintended consequences" somewhere else.
- Seeking quick solutions, or throwing the problem to another group to work on, may not solve the underlying cause of what is going wrong.
  - For example, applying technology to "fix" a problem may only result in ways of handling the symptoms. It does not necessarily resolve the underlying cause. What you end up with is people blaming technology for the problem.
- Training or reassigning people may only appear to solve the problem, but unless the problem is a lack of skills, the problem is not solved.
  - It is sometimes easy to assume the problems are occurring because individuals do not know how to do something and need training. However, pursuing a training solution may even delay finding the real cause while you see if the training worked.

It has often been said that if you find the real problem you are well on your way to finding the solution. It sounds simple, but if you know the cause, you know what to fix. Think about how much time you have spent in your own past trying to find a solution to a problem. How many times did you jump to ask, "What do I do?" instead of first asking, "What really happened and why?" Sometimes after trial and error, the solution becomes apparent. You may have said, "Oh, now I see what happened."

Situation 1

Problem: A manager has a situation where some employees are abusing the company policy of working at home; they are not doing much work, they are not answering e-mails, and they are not returning phone calls. Instead they are running errands on company time and taking care of personal issues.

Solution: The manager eliminates the work-at-home policy. This appears to solve the problem. The individuals are now under closer supervision and their responsiveness improves.

The Aftermath: The truth is this "solution" did not solve the problem at all; *it created new problems*:

1. The employees who were diligent and did their work at home now feel penalized because they cannót work at home. They most likely are not happy with their boss, are upset at their coworkers who abused the policy, and feel they have been treated unfairly by the organization. This translates into less communication and avoidance and anger toward others. The result is suboptimal teamwork and possibly even sabotage to others' work efforts.
2. Action was taken, but against everyone—the honest, diligent employees, as well as the dishonest, cheating employees. The message this sends is that performance and results are not rewarded. Rather, that all will be punished because of the few.

Individuals switch from a "do all I can attitude" to a "do what I can get away with attitude."
3. The honest employees wonder why they lost the privilege of working at home just because of a few who did not follow the rules. This sends the message that the organization does not focus on results and rewards, but rather is focusing on control and punishment.
4. The manager who changed the policy is perceived as unfair, unable to solve or deal with the real problem, and unable to manage employees. All respect is lost. Credibility becomes suspect. Eventually the manager is seen as largely ineffective by subordinates, peers, and senior-level management.
5. The manager is perceived as someone who cannot be trusted.

In this example, no one is fooling anyone. The manager may have taken action to solve a problem and it did. The problem is that employees are now under more scrutiny and cannot get away with what they did in the past, but from the point of view of fairness and effectiveness, the manager failed. So, who was harmed?

- The manager: 1) harmed reputation; 2) lost loyalty; 3) distrusting employees; 4) perceived as unfair and maybe even as less competent.
- The honest workers: 1) punished; 2) inconvenienced; 3) promise of work-life balance broken; 4) unhappy as they adjust. Some may even leave the organization as a result.
- The dishonest workers who may feel the brunt of the honest worker's resentment.

So, what was the right answer? What should the manager have done? The manager should have taken disciplinary action against the non-working employees, based on the company's policy. Since the dishonest workers abused the work-at-home policy, *only those individuals* should have had the privilege taken away from them. It would have sent a stronger message—the right message—to the entire group.

Situation 2

Problem: Individuals who are sent to a training program to develop skills to allow them to be more productive on the job are not getting good grades.

Solution: Management tells the instructors if the students don't start getting better grades they may outsource the training program.

The Aftermath: The students started getting better grades and the system of measurement showed positive results, but months after the training program, productivity still had not improved. Here are some of the things that happened:

1. Upper management indicated they wanted students to get better grades. So the instructors gave the students better grades. That did not mean they learned any more than before.
2. The instructors felt threatened that their jobs would be outsourced. Self-preservation kicked in and they did what they had to do to survive. Grading criteria were lowered and tests were made easier. Remember, management wanted to see "better grades"; they did. No one asked about criteria.
3. It appeared to solve the problem, at least in the short run. Students got better grades. There was a gap from the time students completed the program to the time their productivity could be measured. Making the cause and effect relationship difficult to measure.
4. There was a negative impact on the morale of the trainers. They were evaluated differently, but they were not given any tools or new processes to help them accomplish the goals they were given.
5. Some of the students didn't mind. They could actually show up less and do less work in the program and receive better grades.

Think about it this way, there was a problem that had a number of symptoms. One was poor grades, but that alone was not what made a difference. The fix was to focus on something that could show immediate results. That, combined with the threat that the trainers' jobs would be outsourced, drove the situation to become worse than it was when it started. This should have been addressed by looking at the real issue—having more productive individuals. Once the issue was identified, then a plan could be put into place to look at the factors: training curriculum, student qualifications, instructor ability, etc.

Why Only Fixing a Symptom Breaks Trust

The preceding examples are but two situations where a problem was handled in an unfocused and selfish way. Actions were taken, but the actions were focused on fixing symptoms and not fixing the underlying problem. By not attempting to fix the real problem, the actions taken set in motion a series of emotions, perceptions, and resentment on the part of the individuals involved.

Misidentifying or ignoring the real problem and fixing only the symptoms shows immediate action and may give the *illusion* of solving the problem. *Someone did something and now something is different.* The symptoms we were looking at are better, but the real problem is not solved. Management took steps to do something—at least that is what they say. Unfortunately, over time, it eventually backfires, especially if the problem, which is still unresolved, escalates further.

So, why else is it important to find and remedy the true causes of the problem? Why isn't a quick fix enough? Because, people who lose trust in their leaders, in their managers, and in their peers, will lose trust in the organization as well. The result is they are less effective in their work and their motivation is lower than what it had previously been.

Here are some key things to think about...

- How can individuals have confidence in someone who doesn't take the time to fully understand a problem before trying to resolve it?

- What is the impact on employees when they see a great deal of money being spent (wasted) on fixing symptoms and not solving problems?
- What is the result of managing a department when the staff sees multiple initiatives are not working and little effort is being put into solving the real problems?
- What happens to an individual's credibility when he or she is seen as not dealing with an issue and just stalling until something else happens or someone else takes over?
- What impact do "flavor of the day" programs have on employee support and commitment?

What Do You Do?

Before you do anything, you need to know the scope of the problem and its impact. The only way to effectively deal with a problem is to start by making sure you understand what the real problem is. Use the following checklist to help yourself. You can probably think up more questions on your own that apply to the particular problem or situation at hand.

- What happened?
- Why did it happen?
- Who was involved? Why were they involved? Was it intentional and if so, why did they let it happen? Why didn't they act sooner and more responsibly?
- For example, if someone responds to you, "it's not my job," then ask why the person thinks it's not his or her job.
- Who were the responsible parties? Who were the perpetrators? Why?
- When did it start? Why did it start?
- What contributed to the problem? How did I contribute to it?
- What is the end result you want to see?

When faced with a problem of any magnitude, you need to do four things.

1. You need to start asking "why".
2. Then you need to ask "why" again and again until you find out what the real problem is. Then, and only then, will your efforts to solve the problem have real impact.
3. The next thing to do is decide how to resolve the issues that caused the problem. Rarely is there a single, simple cause.
4. Finally, when you have a solution, put it to the test; you must ask yourself why you are choosing this solution over others.

Think of it this way:

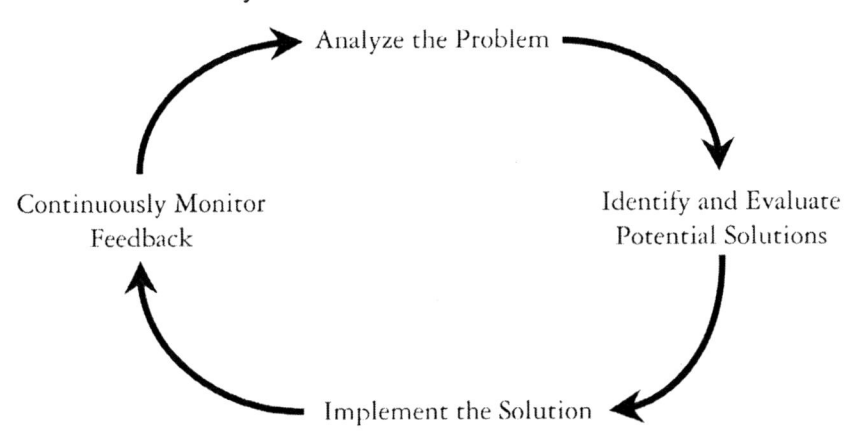

```
         → Analyze the Problem ↘
   ↑                              ↓
Continuously Monitor        Identify and Evaluate
     Feedback                Potential Solutions
   ↑                              ↓
         ← Implement the Solution ←
```

CHECKLIST: WHY DO YOU CHOOSE SOME SOLUTIONS OVER OTHERS?

Are you making your choices based on an emotional point of view (the decision that "feels" right) or on a logical point of view (the decision meets your goals and solves the problem)? While either one could be right or wrong based on the circumstances, if you are making decisions based on reasons *other than what gives the best outcome and solves the problem,* you may be setting up a situation that will actually get worse in the long run, even if there appears to be a temporary solution. Use the following checklist the next time you make a decision on how a problem should be solved. This will help you uncover some areas that have been causing you to both limit and bias yourself.

- Did I choose the solution because it was easy? Was I searching for only the simple solution? We often tend to seek explanations that are simple and plausible.
- Did I only want to "keep the peace"?
- Did I let any of my own assumptions and prejudices get in the way? We often make selections based on filters.
- Was I trying to protect myself or punish someone else? Was I looking for a scapegoat?
- Did I try to only be minimally involved instead of being an active participant in solving the problem? Did I hold back information?
- Did I make a decision and then try to find the evidence to prove I was right? Strange as it seems we often make decisions based on *feelings* and then look for facts to support the decision we made.
- Do I have the buy-in of those that will be impacted by the outcome?

The preceding are only a few of the ways we have seen individuals shortchange themselves when they are trying to decide how to solve a problem. It is easy to let things get in the way of finding the true problem.

Related to "Fixing Symptoms" it is important to realize a significant barrier to trust occurs when individuals do not handle a problem or a situation that is brought to their attention, but instead do things to avoid it. Worse, they may tell someone that they don't have time and the individual should handle it on his or her own. It may be that the avoider is thinking the following:

- "Maybe the problem will solve itself."
- "Maybe priorities will change."

- "Maybe I will end up in another position and someone else can deal with it."
- "Maybe it will all go away."
- "Maybe my other work will suffer if I work on it."
- "Maybe addressing it will bring unwanted attention."

On some level we may feel or perceive we don't need to deal with the situations being brought to us. But when we don't make time for another person we are devaluing the other person. When it happens, problems arise and escalate. Avoidance and insensitivity to others prolongs and increases the level of tension and stress on everyone involved.

Examples

Consider people who always make sure their problems are addressed before they pay any attention to others on their team. They always stress how important the things they are involved in are. What this does is sends the message that "it's all about me" and shows an attitude that says "address my needs first before I listen to you, if I listen to you at all." If this occurs on a regular basis, the other team members will have to pick up for the lack of work these people get done. When their needs are met at the expense of the group and without thinking about the impact of their actions on others, the morale of the entire group suffers.

When someone doesn't listen to us and ignores our concerns, it impacts how we feel about that person. Some trivial issue can become more important than hearing what a person has to say. It confuses the messages he or she is sending to us. It degrades and demoralizes people. It impacts the overall relationship in both the short and long term. *The way we feel about a person is a filter to the message that is sent.* This filter can be either positive or negative, and is influenced by our interaction with them.

A manager fussing over a small item at the expense of a larger issue is also problematic. For example, a company is having its annual corporate meeting and flies individuals in from around the country, yet the organizing manager tells the attendees he is not paying for phone calls back home due to the cost. In the long run such things have a relatively small impact on the budget, but a high impact on how people are viewed. Such actions stop us from dealing with strategic issues. A minor task or decision becomes the focus that clouds the real issue. This can happen to the extent that the strategic issue is overshadowed and even impacted by a minor task or decision that was made on something as small as the cost of a call back home to an attendee's family.

Why Avoiding Other Individuals and Their Concerns Breaks Trust

- Minimizes the importance of another person's concerns.
- Breaks trust because the real issue is never addressed.
- Transfers problems to others who are powerless to help. Ignoring a problem or dealing with too many other distractions makes one look like an ineffective, inefficient, and even an incompetent individual.
- People stop caring and the quality of work drops.
- The person is seen as someone who is uncaring, and employees may not extend loyalty or help the individual during a crisis.
- If the employee is the one who is not handling a problem, the manager may stop trusting that the person can perform. This may lead the manager to take work away from the person and hold back important work or information that might get the individual recognition or a promotion.

What Can You Do?

You have probably heard the cliché that it is not about the destination, it is about the journey. Our willingness to assist others can be impacted by our personal views on where we see the relationship going, rather than how we see the relationship thriving in the moment. As you look at the following questions recall some of the relationships you have had with friends, coworkers, supervisors, and family. Think about how your perception of a relationship influences your interactions with others and how it affects the trust you can build.

- Do you approach relationships, problems, and trust differently if you see a relationship as short term vs. long term?
- Is a problem more important if it happens to someone who is close to you vs. someone you don't know well? Why?
- Does it matter whether the other person works with you, lives near you, or interacts with you only occasionally?
- Do you believe it is up to the other person to solve his or her own problems?
- Do you perceive others as weak if they seek help?
- Is it okay if the other person gets ahead because you helped them, even if you don't get ahead?
- Is it okay to avoid dealing with an interpersonal problem to the point where the other person just gives up?
- Whose best interest do you have in mind when you do things and make decisions?

If we practice avoidance and don't address problems or issues, how do things get better? If someone has avoided your problem, you know how you felt and what you did. So we ask you this one question...

Why and how can you show people you care?

Key Points:

- There are three basic types of problems we encounter:
    - Routine, in the normal course of our work. These can be planned for and contingencies can be put in place to deal with them.
    - Unexpected, due to circumstances that usually cannot be controlled. These require everyone to pull together to share information and resources.
    - Contrived, based on individuals not dealing with or creating problems by not addressing the real issue. These are best dealt with by having a strong network of relationships to help you.

- Fixing symptoms happens when the real cause of a problem is not sought out or addressed. On the surface the fix appears easy. It shows action has been taken and hopefully something has happened. The real problem is not fixed and may continue to grow. When the problem becomes big enough it must be addressed. The issue is that time and money have been wasted and individuals see that there has not been a real effort made to fix the problem.

- The impact on others by not addressing the real problem is that trust and credibility are hurt. Employees often hear management say one thing and do something different. There is a negative impact on teamwork, productivity, and morale.

CHAPTER 4.
HOW FILTERS AND BIAS IMPACT OUR INTERACTIONS WITH OTHERS

Chapter Goals:

- Understand what filters are and how they impact our thinking.

- Recognize how filters impact the communication process.

- Understand what biases are and the impact they have on relationships.

Clear Communication...

Q. What do newspapers, television, and politicians all have in common?
A. They all filter things, and what comes out is based on how the filters are set.

Ever wonder how a group of people can see the same thing and when asked to describe it all have a different view of what they saw and what they think is important? Maybe you have been on a team where this has happened. When it comes to our own personal filters, they can alter the way we see things. They let things we want pass through and they keep out the things we don't want. Our filters are developed from many sources. Some come from our environment, what we have learned growing up in our families and in our respective cultures; others come from the organizations we are part of. Contributing factors that impact our filters are the results we have had, both positive and negative, from our past actions.

Our experiences impact how we create our own filters. They impact how we deal with new situations, often keeping us from harm, but also limiting what we are willing to try. More often than not, it is the negative experiences that can have the strongest impact on us. Remember the first time you came in contact with something hot, such as a stove or hot water? Compare that to the first time you touched a soft blanket. Can you even remember the blanket? Which had the greater impact on you memory?

Research has shown that when there is an emotional component tied to an experience, we remember it differently. We remember it more *vividly*. It has more of an impact. Take a few minutes to remember a strong experience in your past. Now, take a minute to think about how that experience has impacted you and your decision making, even now.

Examples of filters abound. Filters guide how we view, interpret, and interact with the world around us. We create some of our own filters, and we accept and adopt those of others depending on how we view them or the group they come from and our relationship with them. Filters are built from:

- our experiences
- values
- beliefs
- influence of biases
- past learning
- rewards
- punishments
- peers
- family
- loss
- success
- people we associate with
- professions we are in
- organizations we are part of
- education levels we have attained

How a message is communicated and the viewpoints of people who communicate with us also impact how a filter is created. The more people a communication goes through, the more interpretations influence and impact the message before it reaches the targeted audience. This is a key risk in having a message misunderstood.

If we live in a culture of fear, nothing will even be attempted. If a boss says the world is flat and if you go past a certain point you will fall off, not many will go past that point. The few who do are seen as lunatics as opposed to adventurous and innovative. They don't get support and often they don't get the credit.

For a working definition of "filters", consider they are the result of...

- a lifetime of experiences (work, school, peers); and
- tied into our personal value and belief systems.

So, when you say something to someone, know that they are going to filter it through what they have experienced in the past. It will be filtered through what they believe to be true because of the beliefs they hold. The point we are trying to make is that different people can have different reactions to the same situations. If you ask a thousand people the same question, you will get a lot of different answers. Communication isn't just going from one person to another person, unaltered. It's morphing along the way.

Children often play a game called "telephone," it is even more interesting when adults play. It goes something like this. One person starts by whispering a story into the ear of the person next to him or her. This goes on sequentially "down the line" until all people in the room hear the message. After the last person hears the message, that person is asked to repeat out loud what he or she heard. The message is usually very different from the original message that was presented.

MEMORY AND FILTER EXERCISE!

Here is something you can try the next time you are in a group setting or with a group of friends. Have one individual read the following story silently, only *once to themselves*. Then have that individual tell the story to another individual. The second individual then tells what he heard from the first person to the next person. The third person tells the fourth person and so on. Repeat this sequentially until everyone has been told the story (like the telephone game). Have the last person answer the questions that follow the story.

Two men from Philadelphia go on a trip to Italy. On the way, they stop in Chicago. They buy postcards, candy, and a baseball to take as souvenirs. They then stop in London where they meet one man's cousin. Over an Italian dinner and a bottle of wine she decides to go along with them on the trip. When they get to Italy, they stop in Rome and Florence before arriving in Pisa where they meet their long-lost uncle.

QUESTIONS FOR THE MEMORY AND FILTER QUIZ!

How many men went on the trip?

Where did they stop before Pisa?

What souvenirs did they buy?

Whom did they meet in London?

Whom did they meet in France?

Whom did they meet in Florence?

* *Answers for the quiz are at the end of this chapter.*

The point we are trying to make is that this type of unintentional distortion goes on in our work environments. A message (sometimes a vision) is espoused from a high level, but often by the time it goes down the chain of command, the message is interpreted very differently than originally intended. Sometimes the message is intentionally distorted, sometimes individuals don't pay attention and don't hear the whole message, and other times individuals simply forget some of the key points in the message.

Think of the filters through which a message might travel from person to person, department to department. Examples follow:

- The impact of an individual's value system as it applies to work situations, work experiences, and experiences with other employees.
- The ability of individuals to comprehend the message.
- How individuals have seen other people responding to situations in the organization.
- The relation to past company policies and procedures and how they were used in the individual's case. Whether company policies and procedures were selectively or disproportionately implemented.
- How individuals respect or value the person who gave them the message; how the message was delivered.
- The relation to social norms and customary behaviors of the culture as a whole as well as social practices in groups and departments.

In addition, individuals may utilize the same types of filters differently. For example:

- Those people who have long-term goals will likely filter the same information differently than those who do not have long-term goals.
- Some individuals are going to filter information from a cultural perspective, the culture they were brought up in, the culture they are living in, the culture of their parents, the values of

their associates. They may even adopt the values of a group they hope to become part of.
- Some individuals may filter information through their own personal ambitions. They will alter facts to present their cases in ways that support only their own goals.

Our filters sometimes contradict or offset some of our other filters, in particular beliefs and values. Here are some examples:

- Consider an individual born in the United States, but whose parents were born in a country not friendly to the United States. If he is now part of the U.S. military, he is expected to support the United States' war effort against his parents' country of origin.
- Consider an organization's vice president who has been charged with managing a company-sponsored event or soliciting donations for a campaign, when such actions contradict his or her personal value system. Add to it that the assignment came from the president. To turn down the project or to do poorly could impact the individual's chances for a promotion.
- Consider an employee who has been asked by a coworker to "cover" for him or her, for example, when the coworker is slipping out of work early. It may cause a contradiction between the individual's personal values and the importance of the relationship.
- Consider the Olympics and a sports contender who has dual citizenship. Which country should she represent? How will she be seen by individuals from each of those countries? How will the media interpret, report, or explain her decision? What impact will it have on her career?

Now, if that were all, communication would be easy. But there is more. All of those filters that people have are active at the same time. People hearing messages hear them through their filters. People sending messages send them through their filters. And, there are even more complications. People sometimes hear things through the "What's in it for Me?"

filter. And then there is the "Me Too" filter...imagine how communication gets confused when people try to justify what is wrong by saying "everyone else does it—why shouldn't I?"

All of these filters influence not only how we *hear* the message, but what we *do* with the message once we hear it. We filter the message through what we believe are the intentions of the other individuals. What is their goal in sending the message:

- sell
- inform
- educate
- enable
- drive to action
- cover up
- evade
- smoke screen
- empower
- manipulate
- (add your own; the list goes on...)

So, with all the filters the message is sent through, and all the filters the message is received through, what does it all look like?

BARRIERS: Filters

The message

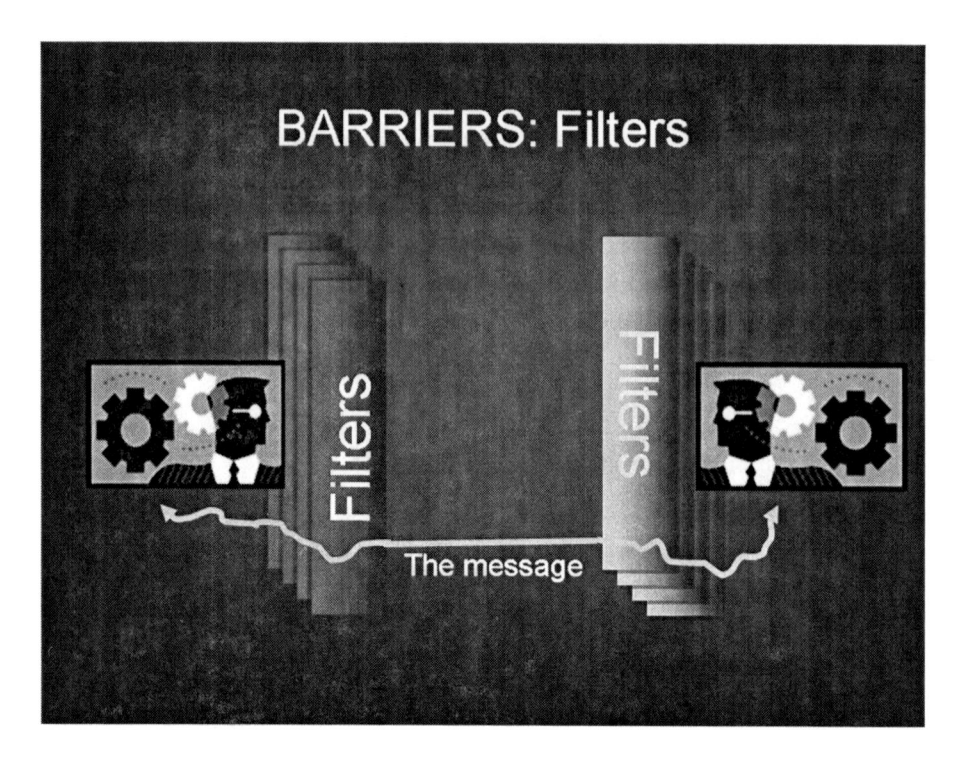

There is also what is called "noise." These are the distractions all around us—people wanting our attention, phone calls, e-mails, and other distractions we face every day. They battle to gain our attention and try to influence us to believe in and do certain things; buy certain products, vote for certain candidates, contribute money to certain causes.

The following true story illustrates the point of how one's filters can influence the way we think and act. A teenage boy's mother went through his jacket and found marijuana. The young man explained he was holding it for a young lady at school. The young man's mother called the parents of the young lady to let them know. When her parents confronted her, the young lady was shocked. Later, when the young lady confronted her friend, the explanation he gave for lying was that his mother would punish him more than the girl's parents would punish her. Think of it this way, the boy's perception of the consequences drove him to lie. Not only did the individual lie to protect himself, he put a friend at risk and may also have caused irreparable damage to the relationship between them. What happened as a result of this experience, in growing up, may have an impact on how both individuals approach life and deal with others in their careers. Who we are is a result of our beliefs, which are driven by our experiences. *Would the boy, knowing he could get away with it, do it again in the future? Would the girl, surprised and hurt, be more careful in relationships going forward?*

FILTER CHALLENGE 1

Use the chart below to list two of your *own* filters and how they have impacted you and a relationship you have had with another person. Look at it both positively and negatively from your past experience. There is no right or wrong, so think about how you have handled these situations and what has helped or hurt the relationship. The point is to see how filters impact you.

SITUATION:

FILTER OR PERSONAL BIAS...	THE IMPACT WAS...
Positive	
Negative	

Filters Impact Communication at Various Levels

If all you needed to know about were filters, it would not be too hard to recognize how you were interpreting and filtering the information you received. However, there are other ways messages are filtered that impact communications. They have to do with the information of the message itself (content) and the medium in which it is conveyed (face-to-face, body language, actions, e-mail, voice mail, over-the-phone, letters, etc.), along with our personal biases.

Think about the following:

The relationship between the sender and the receiver of the message can impact the way a message is communicated and understood. Examples:

- Your manager tells you he has an "open door" policy and invites feedback. That is the message he thinks he is sending. You witness him harshly criticizing other employees on a regular basis when they provide him with feedback. The original message has been filtered and changed by his actions.
- You ask a colleague a question and the response she gives you is, "...Any idiot would know that...." Your relationship with this colleague will determine if you see the response as an insult, a way to avoid you, or if the individual is trying to drive a point home to help you learn. The incident will also influence the relationship and what happens in the future.

Characteristics of the sender and receiver of a message can influence how we hear, receive, and respond to a message. Examples:

- Body language, gestures, and tone of voice can influence how a message is sent and how it is understood.
- Rules, social norms, and the context of the communication either reinforce or weaken the impact and our response to a message.
- Highly technical information conveyed in technical terms can confuse a nontechnical audience. A related example is complex information reduced to simple, but somewhat inaccurate, analogies.
- Relationships between people can influence how the same message is interpreted differently by others. Consider how a teenager tells her father about the speeding ticket she just received.

Would it be different if the teenager were telling her mother, sibling, or peer?

The circumstances, medium, and context in which a communication occurs influence how a message is interpreted. Examples:

- Hearing about a company closure from your manager, or on the news, or by an announcement that arrives via e-mail or on a company intranet site.
- Communicating bad news through a large corporate announcement vs. small group meetings of immediate managers and their staff.
- Giving a presentation that highlights record profits right after cost-cutting layoffs were announced. Compare that to the same situation before the layoff announcement.

Methods, such as e-mail, meetings, and face-to-face conversations, all impact not only the content, but the structure and meaning of the message. Our interpretation of meaning, intentions, and motives influences how a message is conveyed and received. How well we know, respect, and can identify with the messenger influences how we view and accept the message.

Think of any recent major event or public announcement, and then try to recall some of the conversations you overheard or participated in, and reflect on your reactions. Here are some questions to ponder:

- From which conversations do you recall the most content...the conversations you heard or the conversation you participated in?
- What specifics do you recall about the actual event or announcement? How much detail can you recall?
- Did you recall more of the information that is aligned with your personal viewpoint?
- Did you recall information that strongly contradicted your viewpoint?

- Do you support the information and those that are most aligned with your personal viewpoint, or do you honor everyone's individual opinions equally?

Those are difficult questions, but they serve to make a point. Communication is more than just the sending and receiving of information between two parties. We can't assume that because we say something others will understand it. Filters affect the way we hear and respond to a message, and the impact and meaning we get from the message. To be effective in communications it is important to check for understanding with those we communicate with.

How are we impacted when someone disagrees with us, or challenges us? In such instances there can be a disconnect between these things:

- **FACTS:** what we know for a fact (may be based on research, data, and experience).
- **ASSUMPTIONS:** what we think we know (may be subjective, through intuition, or through reasoning).
- **UNCERTAINTY:** what we don't know (we may never have had experience or exposure to it).
- **RELATIONSHIPS:** how we see the other person—credible, dishonest, etc.

In other words, consider someone who is explaining a point of view based on the person's opinion or facts as he or she knows them or what the person has seen happen in the past. If our experiences and education are different than the person's, there can be immediate denial, disagreement, or outrage that could be hard to counter. Yet, getting through to the other person is truly a matter of identifying the filters he or she is using.

Identifying a person's filters is not always easy. In fact, we can often impose our own filters in the process and make assumptions about the other person. The only way to find out about other individuals is to talk to them and listen to what they say. Start by asking not only what their opinions are but why they have those opinions. Be patient and keep discussing the topic without interrupting or being judgmental. Filters can actually set the tone of the conversation.

Sometimes, filters and biases are hard to identify and get through. To explain, try to think about the following and try to identify with examples that have happened to you:

- When we see something happen, we form an opinion of not only what is happening, but why.
- Judgments aren't necessarily based on facts because often we only have the consequences of the actions to go on, not the causes of the action.
- Sometimes people make decisions and then look for facts to support them. This is called "confirmation bias."
- Sometimes, when we think someone is good at doing one thing, we may believe they are also good at other things. For example, John is a good graphic artist, so he will be a good graphic department manager. This is referred to as the "halo effect."
- We tend to remember the last thing we heard, saw, or experienced. This is referred to as the "recency effect."
- We also tend to remember the first things we hear, possibly because our attention is higher in the beginning or we are still thinking about it when the speaker goes onto other information. This is called the "primacy effect."

Why Using Filters Breaks Trust

If we are using filters, whether consciously or unconsciously, why do we need to recognize when they are clouding our judgment? The simple answer is because filters can prevent us from getting what we want, from getting at the truth, from seeing the heart of the problem. Filters lock us into a cycle of being suspicious of anything or anyone who does not pass through our filter check. They cause us to interpret the message before we even hear the whole thing or give it a chance to work. They can block the truth. From the description of filters and how they impact communication, we hope we have shown the many ways in which our use of filters can lead to broken trust. Let's look at a few crucial and potentially dangerous consequences of falling prey to our filters.

Bias and Stereotyping of People

Filters cause us to form opinions of individuals based on the groups they are associated with. Filters allow people to have excuses for not accepting an *individual* for who they are as a person. Biases, which are another form of filter, impact how we interact with others. To illustrate, do the following.

Do you have biases?

Activity

On the left side of the table below we list several types of cultural groups. Go through the list sequentially and, on the right side, write down the first thing that comes to mind about each group—use only two or three descriptive words. You don't have to share this with anyone. If you don't want to write anything down, you can just think of it in your mind.

Group	First things that comes to mind
Republican	
Democrat	
African-American	
Caucasian	
Elderly	
Gay	
Feminist	
Muslim	
Christian	
Teenager	

So, did you think the same about each of those groups? Or, did bias impact what you believe to be true about each group? It is important to know what those biases are and keep those in mind as we work with other people. By the way, if you personally know a member in one of the groups listed your bias toward that person may be different than that toward the group as a whole. Think about it.

Here are a few more ways filters affect us.

- Stereotyping of Organizations, Agencies, and Departments. Filters can cause us to form an immediate opinion of someone just because they work at a particular company, department, or in a particular industry. For example, think of some of the people, companies, and agencies who have been in the news for such things as predatory lending, insider trading, shredding evidence, corruption, and so on. Ask yourself what you would think of and how you would treat a former employee of one of those organizations if he or she came to work with you. Here is another example: what impressions do you get of a person when you first meet them and they tell you their profession (doctor, teacher, accountant, lawyer, salesperson). You may not even know much else about the person, yet you form impressions of them because of the profession they are in.
- Prejudicial treatment and biased interactions. How many times have you done something, or chosen not to do something, based on what you think you know about someone. Do you know a person who shops or chooses not to shop in certain stores run by certain people? Do you know someone who boycotts a particular product, store, or services from a certain "country of origin"?

There can be a challenge in seeing past the "illusion" of the person to the *real* person. To illustrate this concept in a little more detail, complete the following table:

Consider that a close and trusted friend committed a "victimless" crime? (Think of her or him taking office supplies from the job for personal use at home or at school, for example.)	
If you found out, would it change your relationship with this person?	
Which of your beliefs and loyalties would be in conflict?	
Would you try to change your friend or get the person to return the items or make restitution?	
Would you turn your friend in?	
What if your friend got caught and she or he said that you knew about their stealing?	

In this section about filters, we have shown how they exert a strong and powerful influence over us and our ability to see, recognize, and understand situations we encounter. When you begin to identify how you are applying filters and where they are coming from, you will have a start on breaking through this barrier. Understanding why others have the filters they do is a start in helping you understand them and to help you build strategies to work with, deal with, and influence them.

A Process Model to Keep in Mind

To change behavior, there is a model based on the concept of Head, Heart, Hand. If you can get someone to think differently (head), you can get him or her to feel differently (heart), and the result is that the person will do differently (hand). This process starts by understanding why the person thinks the way he or she does and what the reasoning behind his or her actions are. Keep this in mind with the person's personality type as well. Is this an individual who is more influenced by facts and figures or by emotions and feelings? As you get to understand the individual it makes it easier for you to help that person see the situation from a different perspective.

ANSWERS TO THE QUESTIONS FOR THE MEMORY AND FILTER QUIZ!

How many men went on the trip? 2

Where did they stop before Pisa? Chicago, London, Rome, Florence.

What souvenirs did they buy? Postcards, candy, baseball.

Whom did they meet in London? One man's cousin.

Whom did they meet in France? No, they did not go to France.

Whom did they meet in Florence? No one. They met the uncle in Pisa.

Key Points:

- Filters impact our thinking and are based on personal experiences and the opinions of individual and organizations we identify with.

- Filters can protect us, but can also cause barriers to working with others.

- We all have biases. Understanding what they are and being aware of them allows us to manage them in our relationships.

CHAPTER 5.
HOW HANDOFFS, DENIALS, AND DELEGATION IMPACT TRUST

Chapter Goals:

- Understand the difference between positive and negative handoffs.

- Identify the different "degrees of help."

- Understand the different "degrees of delegation."

Handoffs

In a positive situation, a handoff is a way of helping individuals or teams develop new skills and abilities. It can also be a way to help them learn more about an organization, a business, or an industry. From a negative perspective a handoff is seen as a way to avoid or pass off work to others without concern about their ability to get it done.

From a *positive* perspective, a few common reasons why handoffs occur include:

- Giving individuals or teams opportunities to show what they can do.
- Helping individuals or teams develop new skills to make them more effective in their current roles.
- Helping individuals or teams prepare for new opportunities.

From a *negative* perspective, a few common reasons handoffs occur include:

- The work carries a high risk and the one handing it off is seeking to evade the risk.
- The project is a lot of work and not seen as important.
- The work doesn't have visibility and won't get recognition for the person handing it off.
- The individual handing off the work wants to see the person receiving the handoff fail.

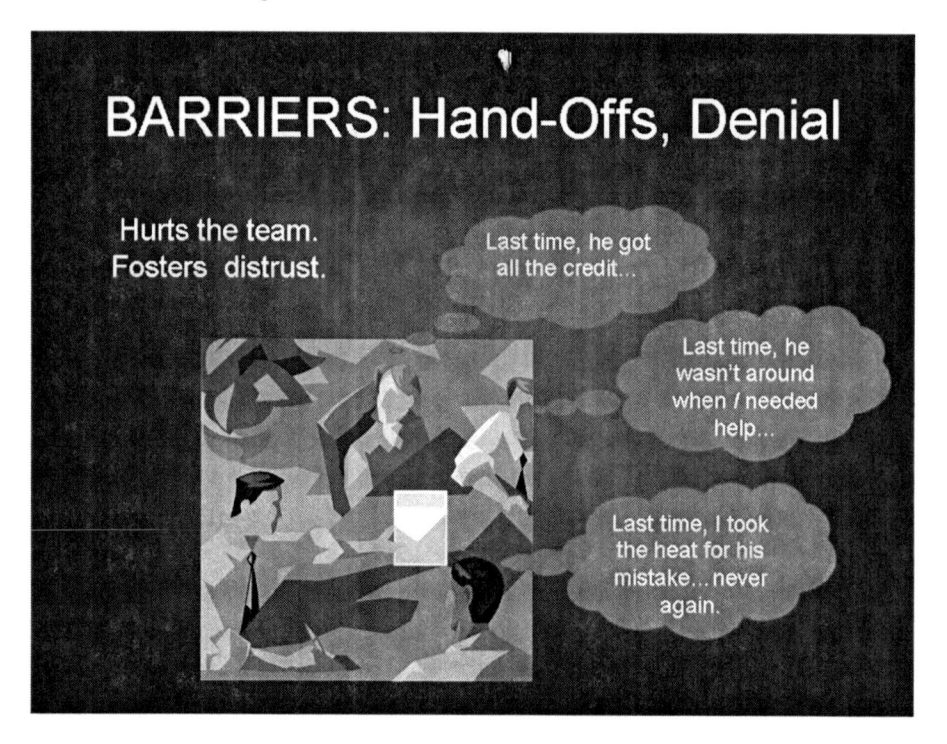

BARRIERS: Hand-Offs, Denial

Hurts the team.
Fosters distrust.

Last time, he got all the credit...

Last time, he wasn't around when *I* needed help...

Last time, I took the heat for his mistake... never again.

Examples:

One type of handoff generally occurs in a process-oriented environment. Here one individual or team completes their part of the work and then hands it off to the next person or team to continue working on. For example, in creating a magazine, writers write articles and then pass their work to editors or graphic designers.

Problems occur when the person or team handing off the work has not done a quality job. The team receiving the work might have to compensate, fix, or kick the work back. The problem occurs when the team handing off the work abdicates responsibility, does not provide support, or walks away from their responsibility by dumping it on others.

Another example occurs when a boss comes to an employee regarding taking over a project someone else was working on. The project went from being a strategic initiative to one that is now considered task oriented and just needs to be completed. There is no visibility, just a great deal of work that needs to be completed within a short time. You have just received a negative handoff (or been "dumped on," depending on your perspective).

Given that such situations can occur in any environment, how would you begin to assess or recognize the situation? Look at the following checklist and think about a time when you were "dumped on." How would you answer these questions?

- What was the work that had to be done and was it in a state where it made sense to give it to another person?
    - Did you know what the expectations were?
    - What had already been completed?
    - What other resources, including people, did you need to do the project?
    - What still needed to be done or redone, which was in addition to your other work and what was the impact on your other work?
- How did you reprioritize your other work?
    - Was the new work additional?
    - Did you have other work you were doing that had to be put on hold?
    - Was overtime needed, to what extent, and how often?
- What political issues surrounded the project?
    - What exactly happened that led to it getting "dumped" on you?

- What type of work was it...high risk, important, busy work, or routine?
- Did you get the work because it changed in importance?
  - Did a more qualified person resign and leave you as the only one available to do the work?
  - Did you get the work, even though you lacked the skills?
- Was someone else trying to avoid risks by passing the work off to you?
  - Did the work impact someone in a negative way? For example, was the risk of losing a bonus or missing a deadline the person's motivation for distancing him or herself from the work?
  - Did someone dump it on you so that he or she would have more time to do the highly visible projects?
  - Did you get the work so someone else wouldn't be blamed for failing?
- Were you given the new work as a test of your abilities or as a developmental opportunity? If so, what support was in place and what resources were available to help you? Did anyone evaluate your progress and give you feedback to assist you in developing your skills?

When a handoff occurs, assessing the situation is key. How can you benefit from the handoff? If you don't see any benefits, is there a way to turn down the handoff or justify that your other assignments are higher in priority? What is the worst that would happen if you did nothing at all?

Something that often accompanies a handoff is "**denial**." Let's look at a working description of denial in relation to a negative handoff, and how it becomes a barrier to building trust.

Denial happens when real issues are not dealt with. Individuals do not face the facts and often manipulate definitions and expectations.

This frequently happens when things start to go wrong with a project. Resources we counted on are not available, competition has changed, or some innovation has allowed a different approach to be better, faster, or cheaper than what we were doing. Rather than admit some other alternative may be more viable, individuals fear being seen as weak or incapable of doing the work so they alter the facts related to the project and its progress. Denial can cause individuals to feel someone has discounted the value of their work or the impact of their accomplishments.

Denial can occur as a result of an organization's culture. You will notice the following occurring in an environment where the risk of doing something is higher than the risk of doing nothing at all:

- An individual's response to dealing with problems is an *"It is what it is."* mentality.
- You hear people resigned to the situation saying, *"You need to accept the culture and not try to change it."*
- You are told, *"Just go along with it."*
- You may hear people justifying the situation by saying, *"That's how it is here—deal with it."*

In many cases, this is where major conflicts begin and escalate. Often, individuals in an organization seek to maintain the status quo. They find themselves clashing with other individuals who want to make change happen. Successful individuals often achieve success by repeating practices that worked for them in the past. Those same practices and habits may no longer be effective, and when confronted with change these individuals don't recognize it so they try to hold on to what has made them successful in the past. Unfortunately, the rules of the game have changed and what worked in the past no longer works.

The impact of this is magnified when highly skilled people are brought into an organization. You may see a high percentage of these talented individuals leave within the first few months of joining an organization because their skills weren't appreciated. When these experienced individuals are asked why they left, there is a consistent theme. In the words of one individual we met, which captures the point very succinctly, *"You hired me for my experience, but when I got here you treated me like I didn't have any."* Individuals we spoke to stated they get tired of hearing *"That is not how we do it here."*

Delegation

Think about the following statement and whether you have ever said it yourself.

"It is almost to the point where anytime a person asks me for help, I need to think carefully before I agree to help them. I want to know what I am getting into and what they mean by the word 'help.'"

Example

As an example, an individual has just completed a report and asked you to "look" at it, but what exactly does that mean to you, your boss, or the requester? Does it mean…

- Checking for spelling errors or grammar?
- Looking at context and flow?
- Verifying the accuracy of data?
- Actually rewriting or reworking the report?
- Taking over the rest of it?

When people ask for help, there must be a clear understanding of expectations. Sometimes we think we know what they want, but in reality our perspective of help may be very different than their perspective of what help is. Let's look at this a little closer, something we are calling "degrees of help."

The point we are trying to make is that there are ranges of help. At one extreme of "help" you may have such things as "sabotage," which is really no help at all. Unfortunately, it occasionally happens, and typically in situations where people feel that their opportunity is based on someone else's downfall or even trying to "get even" at the organization. In some cases, a person may be enacting what they believe to be "justice." Such a person generally focuses on a win-lose attitude.

At the other extreme would be a situation where someone does the task for the person needing help. Depending on the situation, this may be OK. For example, consider the case where someone is just overwhelmed with work and needs someone to take something and finish it. However, we also need to consider situations where this is not optimal because the person needing the help may need to learn. By having it done for them they lose out on the opportunity to develop their skills. Let's look a little closer at degrees of help and situations where help can be positive or negative.

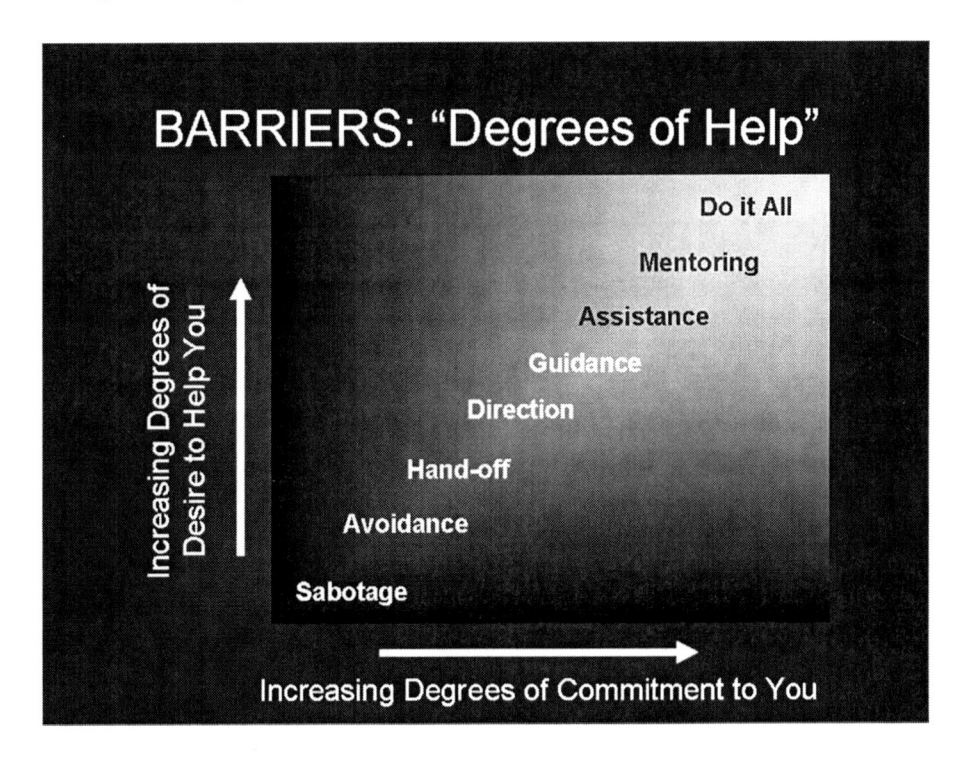

BARRIERS: "Degrees of Help"

Increasing Degrees of Desire to Help You ↑

- Do it All
- Mentoring
- Assistance
- Guidance
- Direction
- Hand-off
- Avoidance
- Sabotage

→ Increasing Degrees of Commitment to You

Type of Help: Sabotage	
Where someone is deliberately out to hurt another individual, a team, a project, or an organization.	
When it Is Positive...	**When it Is Negative...**
Sabotage is never positive.	It is always negative. It is betrayal, and may even be criminal in some circumstances.

Type of Help: Avoidance	
Avoiding a person or situation. Having the ability to help, but not doing so.	
When it Is Positive...	**When it Is Negative...**
Avoidance is never positive.	Avoidance is always negative. It creates dissention and disrupts employee relationships.

Type of Help: Handoff	
Where individuals give work to someone else to continue or complete.	
When it Is Positive...	**When it Is Negative...**
When a handoff is done to help individuals learn new skills and develop it is productive. The talent base grows and individuals can take on more responsibilities and more complicated projects.	When a handoff is done for purposes of evading responsibilities, it has a negative effect on everyone involved. Handoffs are even worse when someone's behavior sets a false expectation that the individual asking for the help will get it. The person asking for help now relies on it and goes on to other things, only to be let down. The person may not even know it is happening. He or she may be set up to fail. Individuals make excuses for not helping, or worse say they will help and then never do.

Type of Help: Direction	
Providing assistance, while trusting the other person will be able to execute the tasks or find out how on his or her own.	
When it Is Positive...	**When it Is Negative...**
When providing direction, you are telling the person what to do, with the understanding that he or she knows how to accomplish the tasks involved. For example, a person may know how to create a purchase order, but needs direction on obtaining approval authorities. Direction provides individuals with opportunities to learn and grow.	Minor, incomplete, or ambiguous direction is not really helping, but giving a person something vague to start with. When a person is forced into a trial-and-error mode of learning, it breaks down teamwork and the person giving the direction comes to be known as someone who can't be trusted.

Type of Help: Guidance	
Providing background on how to do something. There is a process to check-in and follow-up to make sure everything is going according to plan (teaching, telling).	
When it Is Positive...	**When it Is Negative...**
Similar to giving direction, but more focused on helping the person learn how to do the tasks. Guiding an individual includes teaching, providing resources, and assigning a mentor or "buddy."	Guidance can become negative when there is no follow-up or when the guidance provided is insufficient. For example, consider a person who tells someone else, "The form is on the company Web site," but doesn't say where on the web site.

Type of Help: Assistance	
Offering whatever help is needed, being clear about what assistance will and will not be provided. Following up and checking in is routine.	
When it Is Positive...	**When it Is Negative...**
Honest assistance allows individuals to accomplish their work and develop and grow.	Assistance becomes negative when someone "helps too much" and for the wrong reasons. Consider a production department that has quotas on the number of things produced in a month, one person offers to help by taking the "easy" work either from another worker or from the staging area. This helper meets a personal quota but the other individuals run out of work and they don't meet their quotas for that month.

Type of Help: Mentoring	
Giving guidance based on one's experience and insights.	
When it Is Positive...	**When it Is Negative...**
It builds a relationship for the long term. There is commitment to helping the individual being mentored. Mentor relationships can last for years or even decades. Mentor relationships, whether formal or informal, can provide value to both mentor and mentee.	Mentor relationships can be negative when one person uses the relationship for personal gain. When individuals are not prepared to get the most out of the relationship, they may seek the stature of being a member of a program and do little to truly benefit from it.

Type of Help: Do it All	
Actually doing the work for someone else.	
When it Is Positive...	**When it Is Negative...**
Taking over work from another individual is positive when the intent is to relieve the other person of a burden.	Taking over someone else's work, but making the person look like he or she is incompetent in the process. In addition, it may also take away the opportunity for a person to learn and develop new skills.

Of course we would never want to see individuals who are working together hurt or sabotage each other's work, but depending on the circumstances, various *degrees of help* are more beneficial than others.

For example if there is an individual with high potential who needs to learn a function, the guidance, assistance, or mentoring approach may be most appropriate. On the other hand, if there is an individual who just needs help getting a task done and the resources are available to assist, just having someone take the job over and complete it may be in the team's best interest.

A positive way of dealing with this type of situation is, when someone asks for help, to ask questions like:

- What exactly do you need help with?
- What are your goals?
- What is your time frame?
- Is there a particular way you need to have it done?
- Are you stuck on anything in particular?
- What resources do you need?
- Who can I go to if I have questions?

When offering to "help" others, give them the option of clarifying what help they are looking for. It sets expectations. Until we all agree on what the expectations are, we will not be able to determine how successful we are or measure whether our efforts have an impact and to what extent. Building strong relationships starts with clearly understanding what the expectations of the relationship are.

Delegation

For a working description, consider the following:

Delegation occurs when someone assigns something to us, with the expectation that we will get it done.

There are degrees of delegation. Do you delegate the task, the authority, the responsibility, the accountability? Be clear about what exactly you are delegating.

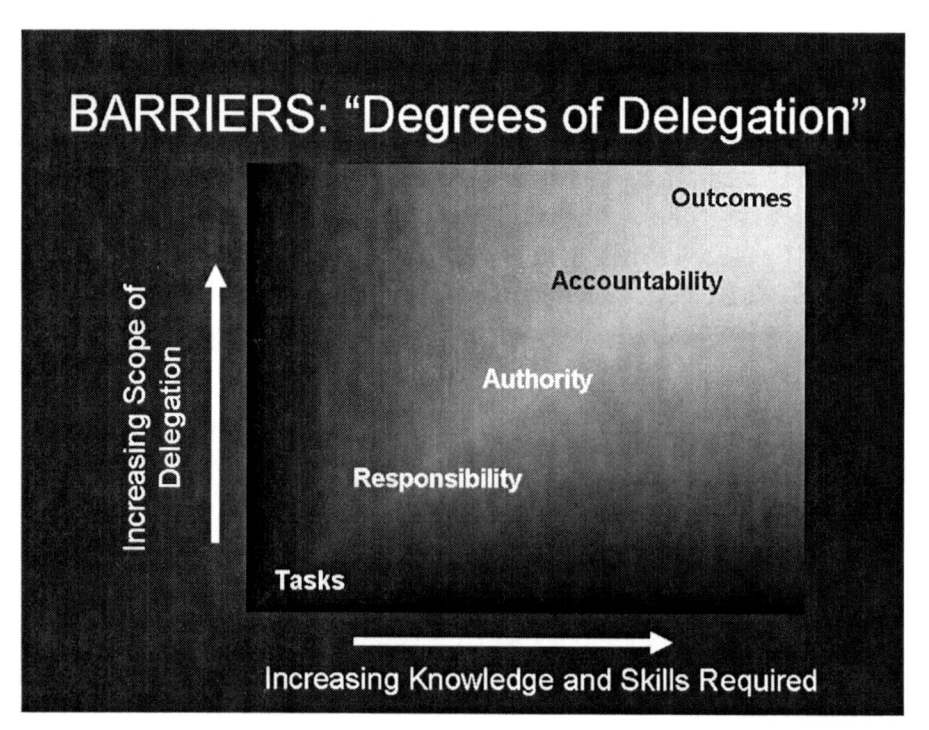

BARRIERS: "Degrees of Delegation"

Increasing Scope of Delegation →

- Outcomes
- Accountability
- Authority
- Responsibility
- Tasks

Increasing Knowledge and Skills Required →

Type of : "Delegation" • Tasks • Responsibility • Authority • Accountability • Outcomes	
When it is Positive... Delegating to others can be positive if: • We know they can do the job. • We want to help them develop new skills and abilities. • We want to create an environment of empowerment and collaboration.	**When it is Negative...** Delegation to others can be negative if: • Someone doesn't want to do the work being delegated. • They want someone else to take the blame if something goes wrong. • They want to have deniability or be able to evade responsibility, but still want credit.

Realize that individuals may try to walk away. The key is to have a clear understanding of who is responsible for what. Understand what is being delegated. Clarify why things are being delegated and to whom. If delegation is misunderstood, it turns into a handoff, and individuals seek to assign blame.

> *Employee 1... "I gave you that job to do."*
> *Employee 2... "Yes, and you didn't give me the tools, resources, authority, or responsibility to do it. You walked away from it."*

In this type of exchange it is not just what is said, but the following:

- What is interpreted from what was said.
- The nonverbal actions that were taken.
- The filters and biases of the individuals involved.
- How the situation was presented, or "framed."

Feelings and emotions come into play, which triggers how individuals see others' actions and whether it is done in a positive or negative way. Fear of failure can also come into play when someone delegates and the other person doesn't admit to not knowing how to do it. This happens for a number of reasons—possibly out of fear, possibly out of ignorance, or maybe even out of arrogance. But in the end the issue remains; an individual is now involved in a project he or she is not prepared or skilled to be involved in, and because of fear the person does not say anything. This begins a vicious cycle of frustration, blame, and ultimately failure.

A handoff occurs when the delegator is not clear on what is being delegated and fails to provide the necessary support. In other words, a handoff happens when someone has power or projects power over us in order to lessen his or her workload burden and increase ours.

If people start working on a project and it is not clear who has what roles and responsibilities there is a high degree of risk. If roles and responsibilities are not clearly laid out, individuals may have different sets of expectations. Often the result is a waste of time and resources due to misunderstanding. Even worse in this environment is that decisions are made based on incomplete or inaccurate data and a lack of understanding related to the rewards and consequences involved. The individuals who delegate work must communicate clearly and make sure everyone understands what the expectations are.

This brings us to the inevitable task, once again, of evaluating intent and motives, which form the basis of trust. Have you been in a group setting, such as a meeting or even a party, where one indvidual stirs things up for the sole purpose of watching how others *react?* Was it to try to draw out differing perspectives? Was it for entertainment? Was it to inject a controversial or contrary viewpoint? Or was it to see where individuals stand on certain issues? Sometimes individuals do this not to explore ideas but to see what falls out and where loyalties are.

Similarly, delegation can be used to assess individuals. It can be used to:

- Test a person's motivations, commitment, or capability.
- See how a person reacts to different situations.
- Learn what decisions a person would make and the reasoning behind their decision making.
- Test individuals under pressure and see how they respond.
- Evaluate if the individual will take pressure in stride, or if the stress and circumstances will impact the person's judgment.

Delegation can be a powerful tool that builds relationships and develops strong teams. Individuals who know they can rely on one another and not worry about others' intentions are better able to concentrate on what they need to accomplish rather than protecting themselves. Trust *begins by being open and honest, and **not** putting a person in a position of compromise, or having the person perceive you have.*

> ## SIDEBAR: DELEGATING WITH THE RIGHT INTENT
>
> When you are in a position to delegate work to others it is important, even before delegating, to evaluate what the potential opportunities and challenges might be. Evaluate the knowledge, skills, and abilities of those being delegated to in relation to the goals of the project.
>
> - Confirm whether extensive guidance and supervision will be required, or if the individual is able to do the work with little support.
> - Clarify expectations, time lines, resources, and measures of success.
> - Have alternatives in case things don't go according to plan.
>
> If you are the individual being delegated to, then it is important to ask the necessary questions to be sure you understand what is expected of you. You need to know the following:
>
> - What are the expectations?
> - What resources do you have access to?
> - What are the time lines for deliverables?
> - How will success be measured?
>
> If the person delegating to you does not give you a clear understanding of expectations, consider writing up a summary of the work and asking the delegator to review it. It may help the person understand what you need and set the tone for the relationship.

Why Negative Handoffs, Denials, and Poor Delegating Break Trust

- Such behaviors devalue people.
- They dismiss and invalidate at a personal level.

- They affect the team as a whole.
- They put people in a position of compromise.
- They fail to develop skills, and create a situation where individuals feel that their work is not valued.

HOW TO DELEGATE TO BUILD TRUST

If you are delegating this...	*You need to do this...*	*and the other person needs to get this...*
Tasks	*Be clear about processes and measures.*	*Directions on how things are done and how success is measured.*
Responsibility	*Allow the individual being delegated to the ability to make decisions (and mistakes).*	*Understand, be willing, and have the skills to make decisions.*
Authority	*Provide access to the resources needed to get the job done.*	*Be willing to work with and understand how to effectively utilize resources.*
Accountability	*Be clear on what the rewards and consequences are.*	*Be willing to step up and be on point for what happens, whether good or bad.*
Outcomes	*Explain what success looks like.*	*Have the motivation and drive to achieve successful outcomes.*

Key Points:

- Positive handoffs can help individuals learn and develop new skills. Negative handoffs are motivated by individuals who want to get out of work, or see issues with the work or potential failure related to the work. Negative handoffs hurt morale, strain relationships, and frustrate individuals.

- It is important to understand and agree on what level of help a relationship will have. Help can range from doing the work for someone who has been assigned the work to actually trying to sabotage the work of others.

- Delegation, like help, can come in different degrees. Delegation can allow individuals to grow and develop if help and support are there when needed. Delegation can lead to frustration and disappointment if it is given to individuals without the skills and with no place to go for help.

CHAPTER 6.
WHAT CREATES TRUST AND DISTRUST AMONG INDIVIDUALS

Chapter Goals:

- Understand what makes a good relationship.

- Recognize fears in relationship building.

- Understand "builders" and "destroyers" of trust.

2000 Hours of Trust in a Year...

How would it feel to spend two thousand hours with people you don't feel you can completely trust? That is the average work year, you know, forty hours a week, fifty weeks a year, assuming two weeks' vacation and no overtime. This is the American standard, but can easily be adapted to European, Asian, and Middle Eastern cultures. Think about it—you spend a lot of time with your coworkers and colleagues.

Before we get started with a scenario, let's think about what we mean by the word "trust." When we speak of trust, we are talking about the type of trust you would expect to give to, and receive from, your coworkers. You often hear the word trust, but it is the emotion and meaning behind it that determine the relationship individuals have with each other.

While it is common to try to separate work life from social, home, and family life, the truth is we spend a lot of time interacting in our relationships with those we work with.

We should be able to expect to have reasonably safe and honest experiences. Let's explore a relationship that was nearly injured by a lack of trust on the part of a manager. Fortunately, for the individuals involved, the issues were resolved and the relationships withstood the emotional turmoil caused by one person.

* * *

Scenario: Let's meet three people who work together:

- *Paul has been with the company for three years and he works in marketing. He is creating a new college recruiting campaign for the Human Resources Department.*
- *Josie is an experienced supervisor in the Human Resources Department who specializes in employee relations and has been with the company for close to nine years. She is involved with the new college recruiting campaign at a review and approval level.*
- *Bill is an experienced manager who was recently hired to head up the employee relations group. Bill is Josie's boss. Bill has been traveling a lot since joining the company and has not had a chance to build a close relationship with his team.*

There has been little interaction among these three individuals, as they are all focused on different activities. The situation in this scenario has evolved over a period of several months, and in this scenario the relationships have deteriorated and become uncomfortable for all concerned. One of the key contributing causes stems from issues of trust, but it was not so readily apparent when it was happening.

The Start of a Work Relationship...

February 12th.

Josie has just met her new boss, Bill. This is the start of their working relationship.

July 5th.

Josie's skills are evident, and she shows early successes. She receives good feedback on her performance. Bill is satisfied with Josie's performance. While they have little interpersonal interaction, Josie's work is accurate and there are no problems.

Bill has, however, noticed that Josie has been working a number of late nights assisting Paul with revisions to the college recruiting campaign he is working on.

July 16th.

It is 5:30 p.m. Bill is on his way home and stops over by Josie's desk to say good night to her, and notices that Paul is showing Josie the new recruiting campaign material. Bill confronts Paul in a half-joking way, by asking if Josie is working for him now.

The conversation continues and Paul tells Bill that Josie's efforts in reviewing the material have been helpful. Josie reminds Bill that employment recruiting is her area of expertise within the company. She assures Bill this is not impacting her other work. Bill changes his tone and says he was just kidding. Everyone writes it off as a joke gone bad, and Josie and Paul think nothing more about it.

July 18th.

Bill sees Josie at Paul's desk, working on the campaign again. He does not go over to them, but waits until Paul leaves and Josie goes back to her desk. Bill calls Josie on the phone and states that he is going to talk to Paul about the amount of time he is asking individuals in his department, and Josie in particular, to put in on the HR recruiting campaign. The conversation takes a turn for the worse as Bill says Josie is spending too much time on the recruiting project. Josie says she understands, says good-bye, and hangs up.

July 19th.

Josie schedules a conference room to meet with Paul the next day but cannot arrange for one until late in the afternoon.

Throughout the day, however, Josie does not know if Bill had called Paul, or if anything transpired. This creates conflict and tension for her. Meanwhile, Paul is unaware that anything has happened and does not know why Josie scheduled a meeting with him in a conference room at the end of the day.

July 20th.

When Josie meets with Paul she asks if Bill called him, and Paul says no. Josie then recounts the telephone call she received from Bill. She outlines what she sees as the major issues, mainly that Bill perceives she is spending too much time with Paul. Then she states her opinion of the situation that is about to unfold.

Paul listens patiently, asking only clarifying questions. When Josie is finished, Paul thanks her for being candid. Then he outlines what he sees as the issues and voices his opinion of the situation.

Finally, Josie asks Paul directly how he feels about what had just happened. Between the two of them they decide to wait and see what Bill will do.

July 21st through 27th

Bill never contacted Paul. However, the knowledge that Bill would talk to Paul created tension between Josie and Paul.

July 28th.

Josie and Paul both notice that their interactions with each other have changed over the last week.

They are concerned about being seen working together so they now schedule conference rooms away from Bill's area.

They don't meet at Josie's desk any longer. Josie does not go to Paul's desk either. A lot more of their communication is done in writing and via e-mail rather than face-to-face. This has resulted in delays and misunderstandings.

> *August 5th.*
>
> *Josie and Paul have a discussion about the change in their behavior toward one another and the impact it is having on their work. They agree it is ridiculous, and go back to the way they were, not caring if Bill brings it up, and both prepare to answer him if he does.*
>
> *However, the relationships between Josie and Bill and between Paul and Bill are tainted from this point forward.*
>
> *It was a question of trust. There was a shift in focus away from the goals of the project toward wondering about appearances.*

* * *

Recognize What Just Happened...

In this scenario, which could play out any number of ways, the story illustrates a key point—tension between people can be caused when there is uncertainty and ambiguity about what a relationship should be. Let's explore what makes successful and unsuccessful relationships, and how trust factors in.

In this scenario we see a new manager, Bill, taking over a group and interacting with the people in it. Josie decided she should tell Paul what happened between her and her manager. An interesting choice given the project they are working on. Looking at the relationship dynamics, was it simply that Bill was concerned when he saw his employee, Josie, putting in a number of hours and being overworked or was it something else? We will explore that very question and another one...what is it that matters in ambiguous situations and why does the truth often take a back seat to what is perceived by everyone involved? We will analyze what actually got accomplished, and how trust was destroyed.

Let's think about the reporting structure, the organization chart. In every organization there is the formal structure that indicates how things should work, how processes flow, and who reports to whom. In actuality, in order to meet goals, individuals frequently work together in teams and allocate work among themselves, which does not necessarily follow the formal structure. When this happens it can lead to misunderstandings. Consider how individuals who have a common cause will work more closely together than the manager and employee in the defined organizational hierarchy. When one considers the reporting structures on the organization chart, it is not the levels and titles that drive getting things done, but people's interests and opportunities to work on something they value. In this scenario:

- Both employees experienced varying degrees of scrutiny by Bill, the manager.
- Both employees felt like they had to change their behavior patterns to be less visible to Bill in order to get the campaign and related work done.
- The confounding factor is that Josie is actually responsible to the company for the area of recruiting that Paul's project falls within. Josie has responsibility for providing recruiting information and reviewing company material in that area so there is a basis for working together.
- The real issue is how all three of these individuals' actions are out of context with the social norms of the organization. We see Josie and Paul performing in what they believe is the correct manner to get their respective jobs done. Their roles, as defined by the organization chart, show a different relationship based on titles. The challenge is that the manager, Bill, sees a relationship and visible interactions that may not support what he believes are in line with his priorities. The manager is not necessarily acting because of the work, but because of the *perceived* relationships.

Recognizing the Situation for What it Is...

This is not an uncommon scenario. Often appearances don't tell the whole story.

Where are the boundaries?

You cannot have trust if the boundaries are unclear. Within any relationship, whether it be boss-to-subordinate or peer-to-peer, it is good to have a meeting early on to talk about what is considered discussable and how the communication and decision-making process will happen. Lay out the groundwork for what is acceptable and what is not. Early misunderstandings, if ignored, can lead to disastrous long-term relationships and negative business results.

Take a Closer Look at What Makes for a Good Relationship...

So, what makes a successful relationship?	So, what makes a stressed relationship?
• Common interests • Similar values • Shared experiences • Comfort with the other individual • Win-Win situation • Mutual benefits • Time to learn about each other • Shared interests • Common viewpoints • Peer relationship • Validation of motivation • Honesty • Opportunity to make each other better • Common colleagues … • Joint future focus • Good intentions • Openness and trust ←→ two ways • Common needs • Drive…want to work and win together • No obligations, no selfishness • Better future for everyone involved	• There is no comfort with the other person • Fear, Uncertainty, Doubt (the "Big 3") • Negative comments about things the other person values • Validation of oneself while invalidating others • Avoidance • Criticism without offering help • Restricted access to information; limited sharing • Feeling of being manipulated • "Company line" and perceived excuses • Me vs. you—everyone doesn't win • Obligation • Devaluation • Dismissal (invalidation, discounting, minimizing the importance of the other person) • No openness, no honesty • "He, you, etc., should just know" • Feeling the need to exercise positional control or power over the other person • Need to suppress, repress others' opinions • Focus on the past of an individual not the future of the group • Self-interest • Interfering in areas outside the professional relationship • How do you fit into "My world" (there is no "us") • Maneuver you out of what you are supposed to be in charge of • Maneuvered you out of the project that *you used to have authority over* • Being boxed in or having limited options • Overburdened by tasks

The key is that individuals who have things in common can openly exchange thoughts, ideas, and feelings and can work more closely and help each other more easily than those who focus on acting the part of the role they are in. Titles sometimes confuse who can say what, as well as what is considered appropriate and what is not.

Recognize Your Reactions

Often, we react to situations before we have a chance to understand them. We apply filters and biases that we have developed over the years that serve to protect us. We try to avoid unsettling situations, which often makes things worse. The key to keeping trust alive in a relationship is honesty, which allows everyone involved to understand the situation and be heard. When individuals' concerns are addressed, they have more confidence in others and they do not feel they have to protect themselves.

A key to building trust is to be consistent and responsible in your behaviors. The following statements will help you assess how well you are projecting an image of a responsible, trustworthy individual. See how well you rate yourself by checking *Always, Often, Seldom, Rarely*.

How Do You Rate Yourself?

	Always	Often	Seldom	Rarely
Your actions are consistent with your words. You "walk the talk."				
You provide the information others need. You do not deliberately misinform them.				
You tell the truth, but do not injure others by divulging confidential information or gossiping.				
You support others and don't intimidate them.				
You understand the interests of other people. You accept the differences.				
You keep your promises.				
You treat everyone with respect.				
You show values that foster trust, such as integrity, confidence, patience, and support.				
You are consistent and do not show favoritism.				
You openly trust people.				

If you find that you answered *Seldom or Rarely* to many of the statements, take a look below to see what might be contributing to fears, stress, or risks that may be causing your actions.

Recognize Contributing Fears...

Often we react out of fear, but it might not be recognized as such. Often, we may just be trying to avoid a situation, but in reality we are apprehensive that something bad will happen. Here are a few fears that can impact your capacity to trust another person:

- Fear of being injured, maybe not in a physical way, but in career options or your reputation.
- Fear of loss, and your ability to recover from a major setback.
- Fear of being the scapegoat, or having your actions and motives called into question.
- Fear of what others will think of you or the things they might say about you.

Getting Past the Fears...

One way of getting past a fear that is holding you back is to identify what exactly you are afraid of, identifying what choices you have, and then evaluating the consequences of those choices. We sometimes think we have no choice available, when in fact, we fear the potential consequences. If we can somehow find a way to alleviate the pain of the consequences or put in contingencies to deal with the consequences, our choices can expand and seem more reasonable.

Look at the table below. Think about a few situations in your recent past when you were fearful or apprehensive, and it looked like you had no options available to you. Look back on all the different options that you overlooked or discounted, and then analyze the effects and consequences of those options. Think through why you threw those options out and whether or not you could have done things to eliminate the negative consequences of those options.

SITUATION	AVAILABLE CHOICES	POSSIBLE CONSEQUENCES	CONTINGENCIES

Recognize What Is at Risk...

Whether you are a manager or not, your individual actions affect those around you. You may never know how, because many times people simply won't tell you. You can go along thinking that everything is fine, but in reality, things could not be worse and your reputation is being maligned.

Think about Bill, Paul, and Josie in the opening scenario of this chapter. There is no way to know if Bill really intended to call Paul and confront him or if he just told Josie that in order to make her change her behavior without really addressing the problem with her directly. There is no way to know if Bill thought Josie would talk to Paul or not. There is no way to know what would have happened if Josie stopped talking to Paul without telling him why. One thing did happen, which was both predictable and avoidable...relationships suffered, work suffered, and teamwork was put at risk.

Regardless of the situation you find yourself in, there is always the potential for little problems to interfere and put the relationship at risk. Here are a few instances that commonly happen:

- There can be the birth of an "avoidance" mentality in employees, especially when issues are unexplained or left to "work themselves out."
- Conflicts escalate and are sometimes never resolved; there is no one to look to for information or facts about the situation and the issues only escalate.
- In some cases, only the required work gets accomplished. Just getting by is seen as good enough.
- Time is wasted when people spend their energy second-guessing or double-checking everything.
- Self-protection proliferates, and needless work is created by requiring everything be in writing.

Solution Checklist

Recall from earlier the destroyers and builders of trust.

Destroyers of Trust	Builders of Trust
• Bad Boundaries • Destructive Criticism • Manipulation	• Openness and Honesty • Validating Others • Accepting Risk Collectively

In this chapter's opening scenario, we saw how individuals perceived and reacted to a workplace situation. There was never any question or discussion about the work product. It was all about perceptions and relationships. There are techniques and practices that can be used to help you. Review the checklist below and see how you can utilize those same techniques when you are in a negative situation.

- Identify inputs into the situation, leading to differing potential outputs. Try to realize what is going on.
- Identify signals, and stay in touch with people in a sincere way. Don't just have a meeting as a delaying or self-protection mechanism.
- Allocate enough time to resolve the issues. Make sure the individuals involved have a chance to present their perspectives. Strive to resolve the problem, not just the symptoms.
- Deal with tough situations; do not avoid them. They don't always work themselves out on their own.
- Assume a role and play it out in the context of the problem. Try taking the other person's side of things and try to understand his or her position and why it exists. Go through a number of scenarios to get the story right. Give the person an approach to deal with a problem. You might consider recording the conversations and playing them back to hear them out loud.

Interactions have risks, consequences, and rewards. Trust overcomes fears and enables us to work through the various "what if" scenarios.

In the end, we all want and need the same things—to trust and be trusted.

When anyone brings you a situation or problem and asks for your help, be open to exploring the situation with them. The following sentences are good ways to initiate a discussion without having the other person feel he or she is being judged or criticized. Remember to listen to the responses.

"How is this impacting you?"
"What worries you about how things are going?"
"Is there something that would help?"
"What are the alternatives, risks, and consequences?"

And finally, think about this...Results and good relationships breed ongoing success, but there is a *right* way and a *wrong* way of handling issues in the relationship.

Right Results	Temporary Success – Cost in time, stress, values.	Ongoing Success – Continued development of people – Long-term growth.
Wrong Results	Disaster – Organization loses, people lose.	Ineffective – Friendships are good, but at the cost of the success of the organization.
	Bad Relationships	Good Relationships

"Mistrust" occurs when you *do not have confidence in someone* or you do not trust the person. Suspicions are raised in your mind about the other person and that person's motives.

Here are some things to think about when people mistrust. You have likely seen such issues in public policy and scandals that have recently hit the mass media.

Issue: Someone in a position of authority is accused of hiding information to cover up his or her own mistakes.	
When the accused is guilty:	**When the accused is innocent:**
It causes people to lose trust not only in the accused, but in the entire organization. Cover-ups can be seen as an accepted and usual way of doing business. Cover-ups may seek to shift the blame to someone else, or to hide evidence to protect the party doing the covering up. The person covering up seeks to create doubt and misdirect any investigation.	The accused is offended or intimidated by the unwarranted criticism. There is unwarranted damage to reputations. It is hard to recover credibility. Feelings are alienated. Vindication is not enough. The person needs validation.

Issue: When leadership and management decisions are self-serving or seen as being hypocritical.	
When the accused is guilty:	**When the accused is innocent:**
Employee support, confidence and trust go down. Employees resort to self-protection. Productivity declines. Retaliation may occur.	People have to work harder to regain trust and prove they are trustworthy. Individuals go on the defensive, trying to prove their trustworthiness. There can be counterattacks and retaliation.

We know that issues will come up, but it is how we deal with them that defines who we are. The key character traits to strive to build in yourself and your teams are:

- *Honesty* - If you don't lie you don't have to remember what you lied about and worry about being caught.
- *Openness* – To truly deal with an issue people need to know what the real issue is.
- *Integrity* – Doing the right things in the right way sets the standard for how individuals will work together.
- *Responsibility* – Accepting the risks and dealing with the issues lets others know they can go about doing their work and not have to worry about organizational politics and being stabbed in the back.

Getting it right from the start allows a relationship to build. Getting it wrong can require a lot of time and effort for the relationship to recover.

Key Points:

- With a new relationship it is important to set expectations around how communications and how decisions will be made.

- Knowing yourself and how you act and react to situations reduces fear.

- Relationships have an element of risk, but by understanding what "builds" and "destroys" trust we can build more effective relationships.

CHAPTER 7.
WHY THINGS DON'T JUST WORK THEMSELVES OUT

Chapter Goals:

- Recognize what happens when people are in an "organizational fog."

- Understand what individuals look for in a relationship with their manager.

- Know what steps to take to effectively deal with issues before they become problems.

Many people are uncomfortable confronting others when issues come up. They hope with time things will fix themselves. The truth is they rarely do. Often people don't know there is an issue or that they are the reason the issue exists. If they are not confronted they continue doing what they have always done. Issues escalate into problems and when they are finally dealt with the damage to the relationship may be hard to repair.

Often individuals show up for work and perform a series of activities. They don't know why they do them. They just do them. They are active, but not productive. They wander around in an "organizational fog." Let's look at a working definition:

> **Organizational fog** occurs when individuals get into a routine and are focused on process rather than outcomes. Individuals don't always have a clear line of sight between their everyday activities and how they contribute to the overall goals of the organization.

Have you ever called someone in your organization for help? When they responded did they tell you it is not their job. They may also have offered to *help* by passing you off (*getting rid of you*) to someone else. Or they told you there is a process that *you* are not following. In the end nothing gets resolved very easily and you do not feel very good about what you have had to go through. It gets to the point where you fear calling to try to get a resolution to a problem, because you know what you will have to go through, the time it will take, the abuse you will have to endure, and the overall stress and frustration involved. All in the hope of getting help.

Maybe you work for an organization that has decided to outsource or off-shore your help desk. Or maybe you have bought a personal computer or other device and the customer support has been outsourced to a different company in a different country. The intentions may have been good—what executive wouldn't want to cut costs by 80%—but then again what executive has to deal with the results of the decision they made to do something like this. Don't mistake short-term savings for long-term costs. A good rule is to put yourself in the place of the individuals who will be affected by your decisions. Would you want done to you, what you are doing to someone else?

There are also situations where one hides in an organization's fog. Let's look at an example.

* * *

Let's meet the players, four individuals who are working in the same department.

- *Eric is the project manager.*
- *Tanya and Marie are the two key individuals on the project team.*
- *Ann is the department manager whom everyone reports to.*

Eric, Tanya, and Marie are all working on an important project. They have many decisions to make, and most decisions require all three of them to be in agreement since they are working on many common and interrelated tasks. Eric has an extensive amount of experience and is recognized as one of the best project managers in the company. Tanya is a solid performer. Marie has been with the company a long time and, while the quality of her work is not recognized as the best, she is seen as loyal.

Marie frequently does not follow through on agreed tasks and responsibilities. She often makes her own decisions, which negatively impact the project and create additional work for the others who have to fix the resulting problems.

Eric talks to Marie about working together and Marie states she is. She points to her work and offers to give Eric documentation from her past work history.

Eric goes to Ann, the department manager, out of concern for the project and explains that Marie has not followed through on a number of critical tasks. He asks for Ann's assistance in managing Marie. At that point Ann also makes Eric aware that on prior occasions Tanya has come to her with similar concerns about Marie.

Ann's response is to talk to Marie. They have been friends for a number of years. Marie tells Ann she will help Eric and the project will get done.

Several weeks have gone by and Marie is still not cooperating with the team. She is making decisions that have a negative impact on the project's timeline. Eric and Tanya have to fix problems and compensate for Marie's work. As a result the project is suffering delays.

The problems have been escalating. Eric asks Ann to assign Marie to less demanding work or reassign some of her duties to someone else. However, Ann tells Eric that she does not have time to deal with the problems and Eric will have to handle Marie himself. Eric responds that Marie does not report to him directly and she does not accept direction from anyone on the team. Ann responds that Eric is expected to manage her because he is a senior employee in the department.

Within two months Eric turns in his resignation. The manager now has to find someone to fill Eric's role, manage Marie herself, and deal with Tanya's frustration.

* * *

Recognize What Just Happened...

While the preceding scenario seems extreme, it is not all that uncommon for one individual to abdicate responsibility to manage the people who report to him or her. It does not always lead to someone physically resigning; however, the person may leave emotionally or mentally and let the manager handle the fallout. Some individuals get tired of dealing with the issues and apply for other positions in the company or request transfers to other projects.

The sad part is that this situation could easily have been prevented by dealing with the warning signs early on. Some managers, unfortunately, prefer to delegate some or all of their responsibility to others and expect that everyone will "play nice together." However, when issues are not dealt with effectively early on, little issues can grow and expand into big problems.

Let's Examine What Really Happened...

- Through inaction, avoidance, or surface-level conversations, the conflicts among the team members escalated.
- Roles, responsibilities, and reporting structure were not clearly defined.
- Who was accountable for what and what the consequences were for inaction were not established.
- The manager didn't have time, or didn't take the time, to address the problems or manage the individuals for whom she was responsible.

- As a result, a poor performer received the signal that there were no consequences and, maybe even from her perspective, no attention to her meant no issues with her.
- Team members received signals too. That they were not listened to, that they were not valued, and that they were not doing well if they couldn't manage another team member.
- The project manager became overburdened to the point that it caused him to leave the company.
- The other team member became overburdened with additional work and left to join another department.
- The problem performer kept doing the same things since there were no indications or any consequences for her lack of performance.

Recognize How Everyone Got There...

What were the warning signals?

- The work was not getting done according to plan.
- There was no established protocol on how to work together to get things done.
- There was no escalation process for when issues came up.
- When issues surfaced they were played down, possibly in hopes they would just work themselves out.
- Frustration set in and work was not getting done.

When a manager ignores issues, gives issues only minimal attention, or delegates the problem back to the person who brought the problem up in the first place, it creates an environment where:

- Individuals do not feel supported.
- Conflict is avoided at the cost of quality.
- Poor performance is accepted.
- Employees distrust management and each other.
- Getting along is more important than getting results.

- Rewards are not based on performance.
- Talented individuals become frustrated and leave.

Recognize the Situation for What it Is...

Aside from any logical or pragmatic reasons that the manager might have ignored the problem (little time, no easy answers, etc.), consider the following emotional context of the situation.

- Up until Eric resigned, he had been handling the project and the problems (having confidence and success).
- It was not until the problems escalated that he went to the manager for help (beginning to worry about the project succeeding).
- By refusing to manage Marie, the manager actually withdrew from Eric (Eric was, in effect, abandoned).
- The message Eric received was, "My manager doesn't care about the project or her people" (feeling upset or even angry).

Recognize What You Didn't See...

Unfortunately, we may never know exactly why the manager abdicated responsibility and refused to manage Marie. One thing is indisputable; the manager had more work to do to manage Marie after Eric resigned. Although we may never know if there were consequences for the manager letting the whole thing happen in the first place. We do know that avoiding the initial problem led to a bigger problem that eventually had to be dealt with.

Recognize What Was Being Counted on...

All managers like to depend on their steady, reliable performers. These individuals can take much of the burden off their managers. A strong relationship can build when managers have trust and confidence in their staff's ability to follow through and successfully complete their work. However, managers can also get caught in the trap of abdicating too much of their own responsibilities to their subordinates. Put yourself in the manager's shoes and try to answer the following questions:

- Would you have expected Eric to handle the situation on his own?
- Others outside the team were seeing the problems, so would you as the manager have considered your reputation as the problems were escalating?
- Would you have seen your actions as responsible for Eric leaving the organization?
- Could the resulting outcome have been avoided?

The manager ended up in this position because she did not have the kind of relationship to understand when there were issues developing. She ignored the warning signs and maybe even thought things were working out. The question we wonder about is, how clear does an employee have to be in bringing up a problem before a manager takes the employee seriously? If Eric had told the manager he was looking for another job, would the manager have taken Eric more seriously? An interesting question.

Recognize Yourself in These Types of Situations...

Don't get caught in this type of scenario. The consequences may take months before they play out and you may not know that the problems are as bad as they are.

So, what exactly are the symptoms and how do you recognize them when you are in this situation? First, don't think, "I don't want to deal with this. THEY should work it out themselves." The problem with that line of reasoning is that "THEY" may not be able to work it out on their own. Don't ignore signs that hit you in the face, and don't hope the problem will go away. The truth is, problems rarely work out on their own, and at the very least relationships are damaged, and in some cases destroyed because issues are not addressed.

Here is how to avoid being caught in this type of situation:

- Look for *objective* evidence that a problem exists, and that the evidence exists to support what people are saying.
- Listen to the allegations. Can the allegations be substantiated? Who did what to whom in violation of what regulation or standard.
- Identify which of your team members and peers you can trust and to what degree. With a few exceptions, employees really want to do a good job, and they don't want to fail or see you fail either. If they feel you will listen, they will try to talk to you about what is bothering them.
- You will see failures, and even have to deal with the problems yourself, but find and have confidence in people who can help you. When people come to you, do not discount the seriousness of the situation. Do not discount their commitment to fix it.
- You will see conflict; determine if and to what extent you should intervene.
- You may have anxiety when you have to approach another person. You may try to fill your day with distractions, being too busy. Don't do it. Handle the problem. Clarify the issues. Validate the people.
- You may lose confidence in the individual that caused the problem. Don't do it. *Involve* the person in the solution. You may have to reallocate resources to put people where they can succeed.
- You will see that people have limits. They reach a point where things go beyond their control. That is when they need you. Train them, coach them, mentor them.
- You may hope for the best and hope everything works out. You may even tell yourself that everything is working out. Don't get caught in the trap. *Hope* is not a proven management method.

- You may feel relief if a key person leaves because it gives you an excuse to re-allocate time and resources to the problem. The problem occurs when you have to explain why you let it happen in the first place.
- You may find yourself imposing more structure on individuals so as to squash the problem or eradicate the issues. You may find yourself asking for more status reporting and progress updates. If you do, employees will have no choice but to assume the extra burden and eventually they will seek to escape from you, your group, and your company.

Recognize the danger signals. What you may not recognize as a manager is that *other* people are noticing what is happening, as well as how you are responding to what is happening. They are seeing Eric manage the problems. They are seeing Eric ask for help. They are seeing you not willing to intervene. They are seeing Eric resign. What does that say about you?

Recognize Your Reactions...

Here are some things to watch out for. When you see them happening to you take action to understand why you are feeling or doing these things, and then rectify it.

- Do you slip into a state of denial, not wanting to deal with problems?
- Do you believe that employees should be able to play nice together? Do you see the situation as being two employees who can't work together? Two people throwing sand in the sandbox?
- Do you feel threatened? Being advised of a situation, is your reaction toward self-protection?
- Do you invoke the big three relationship killers: making someone feel dismissed, discounted, or devalued?
- Do you lack confidence or have overconfidence in your people?
- Do you abdicate your responsibility?

- Do you fill your day with distractions? Is your lack of dealing with issues causing you more work in the long run?

Recognize Your Fears...
Which fear has control of you?

- Are you afraid of what people will think if you remove a key person from a project?
- Are you afraid they will think you can't manage your people?
- Are you afraid your other work will suffer if you divert time to deal with troubled employees?

Recognize the Stresses That Influence You...
Often, we don't see how many forces impinge on our self-control, our peace, and our pleasures.

- Are you overburdened and overworked?
- Do pressures from other responsibilities cause you to not want to "rock the boat"?
- Do you seek excuses for failures, so you can avoid the real issues?
- Do you count on others to divert attention from pressing deadlines to deal with an "unforeseen" event?

Recognize What Is at Risk...

Rewards at Risk
If you work in an organization where bonuses, promotions, and incentives are based on goals and levels of success, people will generally work to reach those goals and achieve the bonuses. In our opening scenario, do you think Eric would have been angry if he missed his deadline and lost his bonus because the manager didn't handle Marie.

Consequences
You may be passed over for a promotion because you cannot manage people and your key people resign. In other words, by your actions you

will be known. If your key people have to continually compensate for a lack of performance of other employees they will become frustrated and burned out. In some cases they may resign, in others, rather than resign, they may give up and lower their performance, miss deadlines, or not care about the results. Such behaviors are not necessarily done on purpose, but are used as coping mechanisms.

Punishments

You will gain a reputation as being a poor manager. Talented employees will avoid applying for positions with your group and will not refer others to you. Having seen the way you managed people in the past may make it hard for you to attract talented people into your group in the future. Successful employees want a manager who will help them grow and develop.

Recognize the Barriers You Are Facing...

- Denying problems exist.
- Handing off problems—not dealing with the issues and trying to pass them to someone else.
- Avoiding problems by abdicating responsibility.

Why We Shoot Ourselves in the Foot

Self-sabotage

Often, we are trapped by our own actions, which are the result of...

- our opinions,
- our beliefs, and
- our values, based on our experiences and the environment we are in.

You will recognize these as the three factors that influence how we filter information when faced with decisions. Don't get trapped! You need to see the problem from the perspective of the individuals involved. Evaluate the situation, measure the risks, prioritize your actions. Make your employees better by being a resource they can count on. Make them want to follow your lead.

Self-interest

If you put your own needs above the needs of your team, your employees will lose confidence in your ability to manage them and their projects. They will lose respect for you and will not trust your leadership decisions.

Solutions – Get out of the Fog...Seek Clarity!

Often, when we are in the middle of a problem, we can't see clearly—we are in a fog, doing what has worked in the past. That is what got us to where we are, so we keep going about our work in a routine manner. Therefore, when you are in this type of situation, ensure you do the following:

1. Be proactive—ask questions and listen to what people have to say.
2. Take all problems seriously.
3. Don't react. Respond by getting complete information. Understand the situation from everyone's point of view.
4. Recognize your filters and objectively evaluate the information you are discovering.
5. Ensure you are not contributing or causing the problem by not getting involved. Accept the fact that your key employees are, in fact, probably telling the truth. Accept the fact that your employees want to be successful.
6. Recognize when your employees bring you problems early, they trust you to handle them—act, take the pressure off your people.

7. Ensure you have established clear boundaries regarding responsibilities of individuals.
8. Ensure you have not abdicated your responsibilities to someone without giving the person the requisite authority.
9. Ensure that when a team member comes to you with a strong statement that borders on an ultimatum, you do not react, but first strive to understand the situation.
10. Work to remove burdens that interfere with your team members working through the problems. If you are asked by one of your team members to assist, evaluate what you can do to help. Don't just push the burden back on them.
11. Monitor the situation. Do not just establish what you think is a working plan and leave it up to the team members to execute your wishes. Reallocate people and resources if necessary.

Recognize that your people are the key to your success. When someone brings you a problem and you see a high risk, you must act. Take whatever time is needed to work through the issues to make everyone a success.

Key Points:

- **Effective relationships are built on trust. When individuals go to their manager they need to know their manager is willing to listen to them and help them.**

- **Individuals want a manager who will be proactive and deal with issues before they become problems. It is important to ask questions, listen to what individuals have to say, and take action on their concerns. Follow up, let them know what you are doing and why.**

- **Recognize that your people can make you successful. Help them through their issues and gain their support so they can help you.**

CHAPTER 8.
HOW TRUST IMPACTS AN ORGANIZATION'S TALENT BASE

Chapter Goals:

- Understand how an organization's talent base gets diluted.

- Understand the impact of diluting an organization's talent base.

- Identify ways to overcome the diluting of an organization's talent base.

People Are Your Strongest Asset

The ability of an organization to achieve its goals is largely dependent on being able to bring the right people together, at the right place, and at the right time. Staffing a department, team, or project requires knowing people, and their skills and abilities. One barrier to achieving success occurs when the individuals who are hired or assigned to projects do not have the necessary experience or skills to do the work properly. Problems arise when individuals are expected to "grow into the job" or "just get it done."

There is nothing inherently wrong with developing into a new position or taking on a new job, and many people have successfully changed careers this way. However, such abrupt transitions can cause turmoil and be harmful when the individuals in such situations are not provided with the support, training, or time to come up to speed to do the work. Let's look at a few examples:

- As a result of new product introductions, a national sales manager has to replace several of her high-performing salespeople who have been promoted into supervisory positions to support the new product line across the country. Does the manager obtain replacements from inside the company and train them on sales skills or does she recruit experienced salespeople and train them on the product?
- A regional manager for a retail chain is tasked with managing the expansion of ten new retail branches in New England. How does he staff the branches?
- A marketing manager has just promoted her key graphic designer to become the art director for a large ad campaign. There is a hiring freeze and she cannot replace her graphic designer from outside. She can hire only from within. Whom does she choose?
- A project manager is looking at resumes in order to select individuals with specific skills and knowledge. He has been given a certain limit on salaries, which are too low to attract individuals with adequate experience, either internal or external. How will he staff the project?

These are typical scenarios that have one thing in common. The positions require specialized knowledge and skills. In today's work environment, projects, quotas, and deadlines do not necessarily change just because of staffing challenges. Individuals facing such decisions can hire the best people they can, and then support them through mentoring, coaching, and training to help them come up to speed.

Impact on People

Now, let's look at the other side of the situation and examine what happens when people are replaced for the wrong reasons, or the wrong person is recruited to fill a job based on something other than talent and experience. Over time this can have a major impact on the overall organization.

Diluting an organization's talent base begins when managers start hiring people for reasons other than their ability to do the job. The question is, "Why would anyone 'dilute' an organization's talent base?" It has to do with gaining and maintaining power and control. It is not about the quality of the work, but about the image portrayed related to the work.

Consider the following example: an individual is hired into an organization and goes along for a few months; getting a feel for how things work, learning processes and how people interact with each other. This is often referred to as the "entry" or "honeymoon" stage. As she gains experience she starts to see things differently. She enters the "feeling out" stage. She begins to question things more critically. She may even take some risks or unknowingly do something a manager disapproves of. She feels there is a better way and tries to change things. It may begin to feel like a tug of war that begins a "downward cycle" where individuals feel dragged down by others in the department who just go along with the "system." This leads to the "settling in" stage. Individuals either find their roles and see how their initiatives will be rewarded or decide that their efforts will not be rewarded at all; as a result, they emotionally disengage from the job. Productivity suffers and individuals seek a way to "get by" rather than perform. Depending on the circumstances and degree of pain, the individual may begin to look for a way out and move into the "change" stage. Unfortunately, some people spend entire careers going through this cycle again and again.

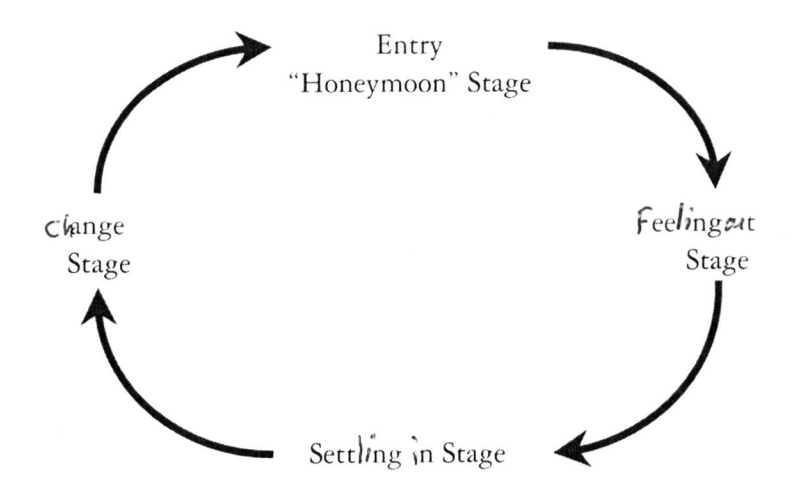

Entry "Honeymoon" Stage → Feeling out Stage → Settling in Stage → Change Stage → (cycle repeats)

When individuals focused on being strategic and innovative are put in an environment where a number of individuals have been hired solely on their supporting a manager's agenda, it results in turmoil and eventually turnover. This leads to lost productivity and higher costs in continually bringing new individuals into the organization. Things such as the expense of training, cost of lost productivity, and lost customer confidence, can all negatively impact the morale of other individuals as well as an organization's ability to reach its goals. Managers often come out looking good for coping with this cycle of events, yet often they are the ones who created the situation in the first place.

Let's look at a few specific situations where dilution occurs. As you read the examples, try to think of situations you have seen that are similar.

- Managers hire individuals with the intent of making their own lives easier, rather than hiring individuals who might challenge the status quo and drive innovative change. Established managers have a power and comfort level they want to maintain. Control becomes the key and self-preservation the goal.
- Managers hire someone because they like the person, even though they may not have fully determined if he or she has the requisite skills to perform the job.
- Managers hire individuals who have no experience in the job function; they're hired because they have worked in the company for a long time and know how to "work the system."
- Managers hire individuals without the necessary educational background and experience to replace skilled professionals.
- Managers hire individuals who are highly skilled, but in areas that don't apply to the job they have open.

The manager is actually setting in place a negative spiral that might not have consequences until months later. Here is what happens. As the number of individuals with the needed knowledge, skills, and capability declines, the skills they possess *as a group* also decline. The total work a department has to perform is based on it having a certain skill set.

However, the manager does not compensate by changing workloads, or schedules. While it is possible to improve and do "more with less," at some point you simply cannot do any more and you get less out of the people you have. Overloading your employees leads to frustration, issues with quality, morale, and turnover.

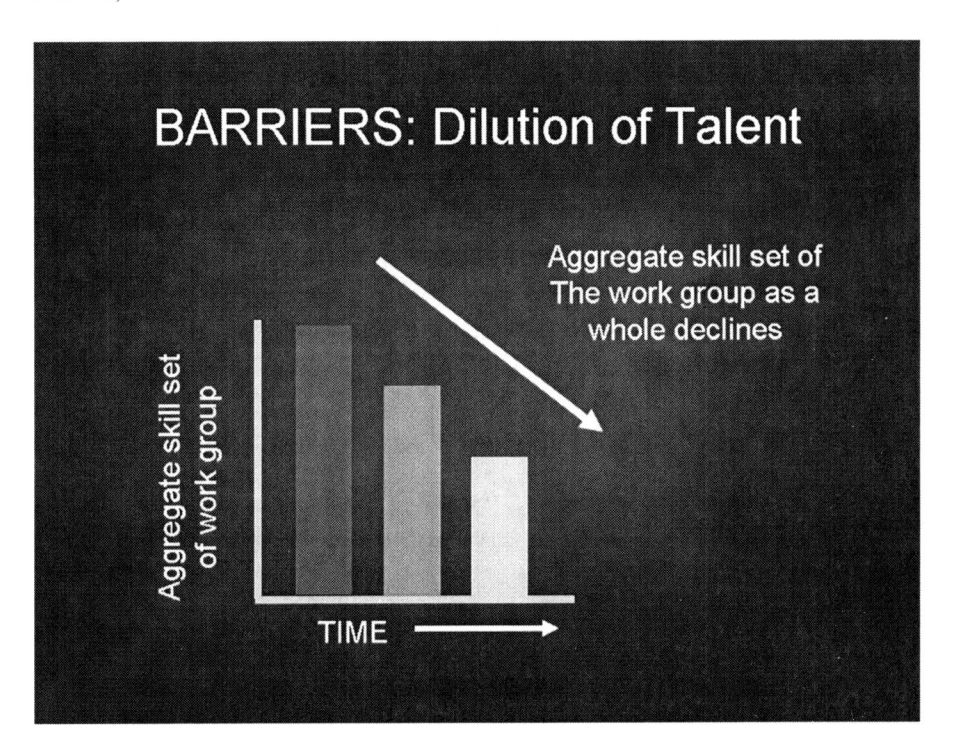

BARRIERS: Dilution of Talent

Aggregate skill set of The work group as a whole declines

Aggregate skill set of work group

TIME

Done often enough, the demographics of the department and the attitude of the workforce change. The department may not get the same production level. The skilled individuals may come to resent the fact that people are being replaced for reasons that have little to do with their ability to do the job. The new individuals may be viewed as people who...

- Cannot do the job properly or accurately.
- Rely on the skilled people and get credit for work they did not do.

- Burden existing employees and negatively impact existing employees' performance.

The point we are trying to make is that this type of behavior happens a lot. Think of a time when you have witnessed someone get a job, but there were better qualified people available (maybe you). Then answer the following questions:

- What did it do to the work environment?
- What impact did it have on the team and the individuals involved?
- How did it impact existing relationships?
- How were the new people viewed? Were they welcomed?
- What happened to the quality of the work?
- What impact did it have on the level of effort individuals made?
- What did it do for the reputation of the organization?

If it happened to you, how did it make you feel?
If it happened to a friend or colleague, how did you feel about that?

Why Diluting the Talent Base Breaks Trust

- Sends a message that the manager does not value the skills of the individuals in the department.
- Places a greater burden on the experienced staff or other highly skilled people who have to make up for the lack of skills in the new people.
- Increases stress as those unable to do the job will have to work harder, and experienced people will spend more time teaching, mentoring, and picking up the slack.
- The manager loses credibility, and is seen as someone who cannot hire the right people, and it is not because the right people are unavailable.

- Quality and productivity decline and it takes more time to accomplish tasks.

What Can Be Done?

- Define the competencies (knowledge, skills, abilities) required for the position.
- Check (benchmark) market data to determine what these positions require at other organizations and what market salary rates are.
- Implement an effective skills assessment during the hiring process; conduct a skills evaluation to determine what development may be needed. This will also allow you to see how closely an employee's skills meet the needs of the position.
- Provide individuals with a skills development plan and a process to allow them to develop the skills they need to do the job.
- Put in place a plan for frequent progress checks to ensure the new person progresses and does not struggle. Feedback is key.
- Assign individuals to assist the new person, but ensure you assign specific and limited scope for that assistance. Work out a plan between the new and existing employees to set expectations, so everyone knows what is required.
- Understand that the learning curve and assistance provided can impact the workload while the new person gets up to speed.
- Don't punish individuals when they struggle or make errors as they learn the new job.
- In the short term evaluate effort, in the long term results.

If you are in a position that determines who is selected for the talent base, keep in mind the impact and consequences diluting it will have. If you unfortunately are stuck having to work with the decisions of others, here are some things to keep in mind:

- Evaluate whether the person wants to learn the skills to be successful. If so, help the person develop successfully. If not, determine a way to keep him or her from demoralizing others.
- Determine what organizational or process changes can be put in place to overcome any negative impact on quality and production.
- Set expectations, let individuals see how their decisions and actions impact the team as a whole. Use the opportunity to provide feedback and build on lessons learned rather than as a tool to punish and blame.
- Look to see if your area can be restructured to work more effectively.
- Look to your business partners to see if and how they can help you.
- Reevaluate and reprioritize projects.
- Bring the team together and explain the challenges. Give the team an opportunity to have input in how to deal with the challenges.

As a member of any group, you have an obligation to work together—not just to meet a deadline or finish a task or project, but to work with each other and help make everyone successful.

Key Points:

- An organization's talent base can be diluted either intentionally or by circumstances. Intentional dilution occurs when individuals seek to gain control over a group and the people in it. Power and control become more important than productivity and quality.

- Diluting an organizations talent base results in increased turmoil and individual frustration. Eventually members of the group look for a way out. When circumstances drive the dilution it is important to look at the goals of the group and strategize on what and how goals will be achieved.

- To overcome diluting an organization's talent base, begin by realizing what is happening and the potential impact it can have on a group. An understanding of the motives of the individuals involved and what they want to accomplish helps put things in perspective.

CHAPTER 9.
RECOGNIZING CONTROLLING BEHAVIORS

Chapter Goals:

- Identify the dimensions of control.

- Understand the positive and negative aspects of control.

- Be able to identify potential consequences of controlling behaviors.

- Understand the dimensions of management.

It's about Boundaries

Employee – "Trust me," she said.
Coworker – "OK," he said ("But, only so far," was what was on his mind).

No, it's not a dialog from a bad movie. But, it is a situation we can all relate to. When it comes to building trust, there is one characteristic that always gets in the way—our desire to be the masters of our own destiny.

One characteristic that impacts nearly everything that happens in our professional or personal relationships is the degree to which we need to exercise control over the environment and people around us, and how we do it. In this chapter we hope to show how exercising control over situations, but not individuals, actually increases the level of trust others have in us.

A Closer Look at Control

For a working description, consider the following four dimensions of control:

Gaining Control: Having the knowledge and experience or willingness to learn what is needed to do the tasks at hand. Being confident in our ability to find resources and alternatives when we don't have everything we need or when things go wrong. Learning or inventing processes that ensure success.

Having Control: Accepting the situation *as it is*, and not how we think it should be. Not seeking blame, but rather seeking to understand the circumstances and events that led up to a situation. Identifying the true causes and finding the remedies. Being able to function effectively in the environment we are in. Uncertainty is dealt with as it comes up.

Exercising Control: Understanding that people have varying perspectives on how much control they need over the events in their life. Managing the situation so people know what has to be done, and the steps needed to get it done. Meeting the needs of others in order to accomplish our objectives.

Maintaining Control: Letting people know what needs to be accomplished. Aligning everyone's expectations *as the situation changes*. Managing the obstacles and boundaries that get in everyone's way. Supporting people while they strive to meet expectations. Never needing to seek blame, but assuming responsibility and accountability for what is under our control. Administering rewards and punishment to get things done.

From the prior dimensions, it is clear we do not mean controlling what other people are allowed to say, do, think, or feel. We do not mean establishing a "rule book" of *should's*, *ought to's*, and *must not's*. We mean one simple thing that goes far toward inspiring others to trust you and you to trust yourself – building quality relationships.

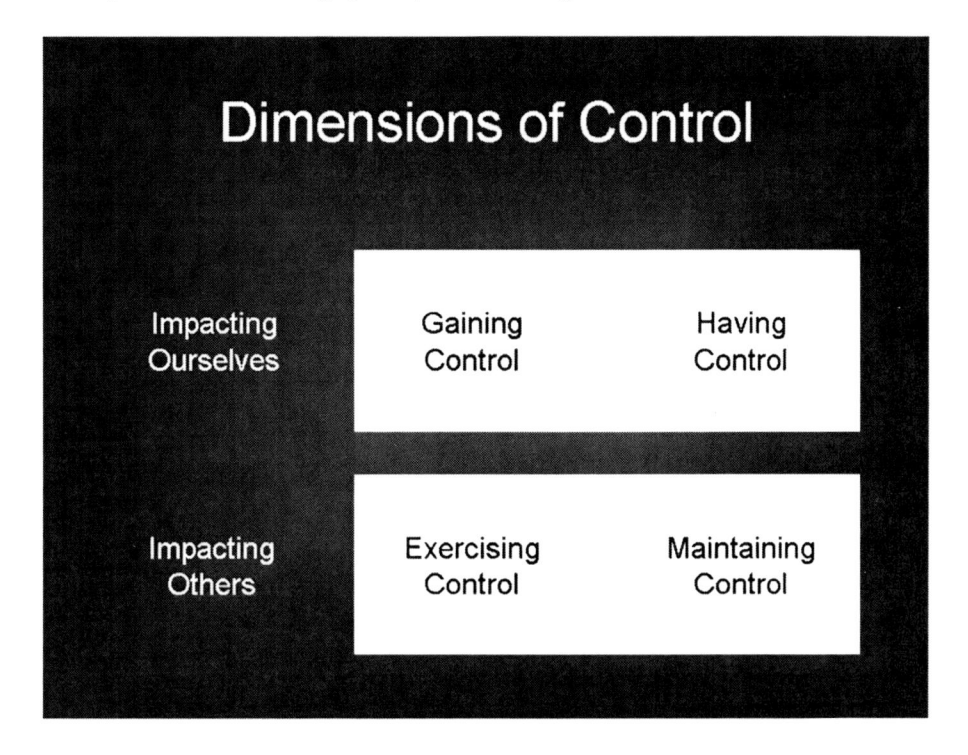

Dimensions of Control

Impacting Ourselves	Gaining Control	Having Control
Impacting Others	Exercising Control	Maintaining Control

If you look at our description of maintaining control, it implies you may be doing things you don't think you should have to, or doing things you expect other people to just do on their own. Unfortunately, people don't always do things on their own. They rely on you, as the person managing the situation, tasks, or project, to direct them. It is all in how you control the situation. Before we get to the specifics of how to do that, let's look at how an individual might respond to someone else trying to exercise control over them and how the actions impact the level of trust in the relationship.

Controlling Behaviors—Putting Them in Perspective

Have there been times in your life when you have felt in control, out of control, or under someone else's control? If you are like us, you have probably had those feelings when people have crossed some boundary and tried to control *you*—as an individual. Sometimes with our consent, sometimes against our will.

Based on the situation, you may have felt victimized, or in a position where you felt you had no other viable choices in the matter. Look at the following table and recall some recent experiences in your personal or work life. How did you feel? How did you react?

When things like this happen to you...	*What do you feel and what do you do...* *If it happens at work?* *If it happens at home?*
Someone made a decision for you, without your consent or input.	
Someone influenced your decisions, without your asking them for advice.	
Someone scheduled your time without consulting you, or "volunteered you" to do something without your knowledge or consent.	
Someone questioned your actions or your motives.	
Someone offered help, but didn't follow through on helping, or did it wrong.	
Someone asked you for help, but was unclear on the details and then put the blame on you when things went wrong.	

Someone imposed on your time or showed up unexpectedly.	
An unexpected problem occurred and you were the only one who could fix it.	

So, after looking at these events, do you feel a struggle for control? Chances are, given the same type of situations, you would respond differently based on who is involved. If they occur at work, you may be less annoyed if it were your boss and more annoyed if it were another employee who did it. If it were family, you may have reacted differently than if it were a neighbor or a casual friend. Chances are you also may have noticed the following:

- In some instances you feel like someone is trying to control you, in other situations you may feel there is a mutual agreement on what needs to be done.
- In some of the situations, you feel you have control, and in others you feel out of control.
- In some situations, you agree with what the other person wants, and in others you go so far as to be resentful.
- Depending on the circumstances and the individuals involved, you may be happy to help. In other situations you may protest or even refuse.

What we have tried to show is that how we respond to the actions of other individuals when they try to control various aspects of our life depends on:

- The individuals involved and our relationship with them.
- Our need to feel we have some amount of control over our own lives, and our need to exercise control over others.
- The situation we are involved in and what is at risk.

- How much we know about the context of the situation and the other person's intentions.

Breakdowns in trust occur when we find ourselves in situations where someone else is trying to control or influence *what we say, do, think, or feel*—and not just control the *situation* itself. We begin to question their motives. We begin to protect ourselves from being hurt.

Positive and Negative Sides of Control

As you probably surmised after going through the above exercise, there are times when people exercise control in a positive way and also in a negative way. Who wins? Who loses? Let's take a look and see. Earlier, we wrote about the three keys to building trust, and three behaviors that destroy trust. Here they are again.

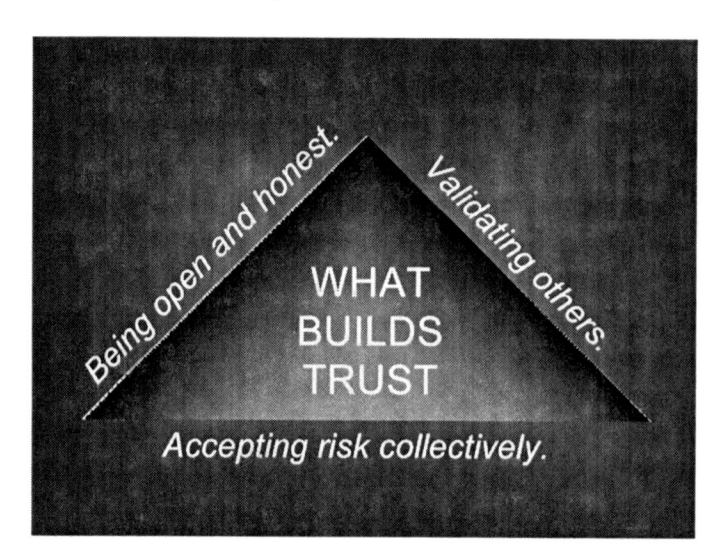

Being open and honest.
Validating others.
WHAT BUILDS TRUST
Accepting risk collectively.

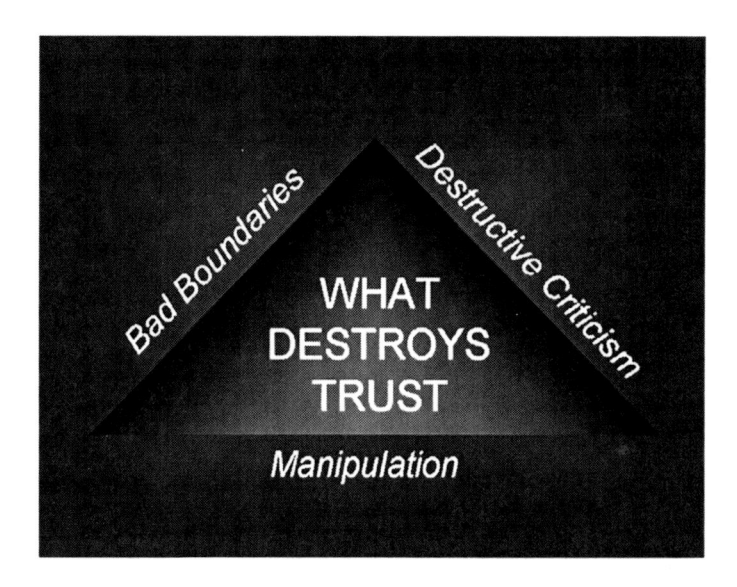

WHAT DESTROYS TRUST
- Bad Boundaries
- Destructive Criticism
- Manipulation

When we look at what influences trust, we see that the degree to which individuals try to control other individuals can have a positive or negative impact on the relationship. In other words...

- There are *positive* ways and *negative* ways of exercising control.

POSITIVE WAYS OF EXERCISING CONTROL	NEGATIVE WAYS OF EXERCISING CONTROL
On the positive side, exercising control in an effective way can help build trust between individuals.	On the negative side, misusing or abusing control can destroy trust, even among close friends.
• The ability to effectively control situations and events allows us to have a plan and act accordingly.	• Trying to control the behaviors and attitudes of others can cross *personal boundaries*. This occurs when we intrude on them without regard for their opinions, rights, or needs.

• Maintaining composure and being in positive control during any situation enables others to see that we are seeking a solution to the problem, and not just looking for recognition. By our efforts to help and validate others, we enable them to work with a solution-based focus, and build the desire to work with us, not against us. We all work toward a shared goal (for the better) not on different agendas (for the worse).	• The need to control can also cause us to be insecure in our own actions. When we are unsure of ourselves, we can create insecurity in the people around us. Individuals begin to distrust how the situation is being managed, and begin to criticize people around them. This does nothing to make the situation better, and makes it harder to work together. Suspicions and doubts arise, and effectiveness suffers.
• Effective use of control improves the ability of the team and organization to confidently deal with risks and consequences. As a leader, you are perceived as an individual who can be trusted to work for the good of everyone involved. Stress and anxiety on the team can be diffused when there is evidence that things are not out of control and individuals are not being sought out to blame.	• When control is exercised beyond what is needed to contain and manage a situation, people come under undue pressure and stress. They begin to look for ways around the situation, ways they can manipulate things to relieve the stress. In doing so they may alienate others.

Clearly then, if there are positive and negative ways to control situations, there are positive and negative consequences as well.

Consequences of Controlling Behaviors

Regardless of whether one has authority over another person or not, consider that all of us *knowingly or unknowingly* can do things that:

- hurt other people's feelings;
- cause other people harm;
- create social norms that team members resent or resist; and
- create environments where people mistrust each other.

Look at the following examples and notice how, on the surface, these types of behaviors don't appear to be ways of controlling others. But in reality, they are and they create barriers to interpersonal relationships and team cohesiveness. In these examples, adapted from real experiences, the people involved employed tactics to better control their circumstances, but they did so at other individuals' expense. Much of it is not deliberate, but the effects still have a negative impact on others.

Example 1: Sometimes what we say about another person is more of a reflection on us than on the person we are talking about. Consider the following:

- *Connie is having a conversation with her manager, Agnes, about work. For no apparent reason, or for reasons known only to Connie, the conversation shifts. Out of the blue she tells Agnes about a time when another person (who also reports to Agnes) got so mad that she left a fellow worker stranded at the airport. Now, ask yourself, why did Connie feel a need to reveal that? It had nothing to do with the conversation at hand. How would such a conversation impact your ability to trust the individual who said it?*
- *Jason told his manager, Tom, that he was going to interview an internal candidate for a position. Tom made it a point to recount a tragedy in the candidate's family some time ago. Why would he change the subject? It had nothing to do with the candidate's ability to do the job. Was he trying to influence a decision?*

In these examples things were said to create an image of someone. Was there an intent to prejudice opinions? Were Connie and Tom trying to create a bias? Were they trying to secure a better relationship by confiding negative details about others? Maybe none of these. But, if you were Jason, would you trust what Tom might say about you, or would you wonder about his loyalty? Based on this, if you were Agnes, would you be able to trust Connie with confidential information in the future?

Example 2: A team member, manager, or even a coworker can require individuals to perform processes or procedures that are seen as punishing or unfair. It is not uncommon for individuals to use varying control tactics to show they have control over their people, their department, or a situation they are involved in. Some would argue that these are sound management practices. However, what is happening is that someone is forcing a decision on others, instead of directly confronting the real problem. They are using controlling tactics that in the long term destroy trust. Take a look at the following situations and decide for yourself.

- A branch office makes a change so everyone has to start at 8:00 a.m. because a few people abused the privilege of flexible work hours.
  Perceived Problem: Staff not honoring a privilege, so the privilege is taken away.
  Real Problem: A few individuals are abusing a privilege.
  Control Tactics at Work: Punish everyone for the actions of a few.
  Real Solution: Handle the situation with the individuals who are abusing the privilege.
- An office in one company allows telecommuting, but in another office they adhere to a rigid time schedule and disallow telecommuting.
  Perceived Problem: Staff needs to be on the premises to do their work.
  Real Problem: Burden resulting from added time and effort to coordinate and manage remote employees.
  Control Tactic at Work: Strict rules and guidelines are enforced.
  Real Solution: Implement communication and work practices that address issues when people are working remotely. Try

working with the other office to find out how they make it work and deal with the issues that come up.
- A person in one department refuses to assist a new employee because it is not listed in her job description.
   Perceived Problem: The individual feels it is not her job to help new employees. She had to learn how to survive on her own and so should they.
   Real Problem: Burden resulting from the additional work that comes with bringing a new employee on board.
   Control Tactic at Work: The experienced individual does not see that the person being hired could help her at some point so she adopts a "sink or swim" attitude and leaves the new employee on his own.
   Real Solution: Create a culture of "support." Show individuals how they will benefit by helping others get up to speed more quickly.

As you can see from these scenarios, when someone makes decisions and creates rules that others must adhere to it begins a negative spiral that can get passed on throughout the organization. Often it is hard to trust someone who solves problems by avoiding the real issue and doing what is either easy or convenient rather than doing what is right.

Example 3: This control tactic is hard to recognize, because we would like to believe others are not out to use us. Coming under the pretext of friendship, some employees are nice to us just to see what we know or how we feel about a certain person or issue.

Imagine you are new to a project and another person wants to find out what you think of management, another team member, or a client. The conversation leans toward hypothetical questions. "What do you think a good manager should do in the situation?" or "You saw the proposal, what did you think of it?"

Remember, when you respond to a hypothetical question, you are really giving your opinion to another person about a real situation. Nothing is "off the record." The other person can take what you say about the hypothetical situation and misapply it to the real question he or she wants answered. Here's an example:

> Robert works in a large marketing department and is thinking... *"I am looking for a new administrative assistant and I am thinking about Margaret, who works for Carol in one of the other departments. But, I don't know how well Margaret handles her duties."*
> Robert asks Carol... "Can you help me? I am working on a process improvement project for the administrative group in my department. Have you had any issues with your people that I can learn from? Can you suggest things we can do to make our administrative staff more effective?" Can you tell me how effective your administrative assistant is?

From the question, Carol would naturally think Robert is asking for help in solving some problems related to how his administrative group functions. Carol begins to tell Robert about events and situations and mentions how Margaret, her administrative person, was having trouble handling them. By suggesting ways of improving the process, Carol is trying to help Robert with his processes; however, Robert wants to find out about Margaret's flaws. Robert asks one question, but is looking for an answer to a different one.

Example 4: When a few people help too many people too often, they can create an environment of "dependence." A similar situation occurs when one person relies on another person who knows a lot about a department or function in the company. The impression is that he or she is the only one who can do it right. Unfortunately, there are negative effects:

- People are not developed or cross trained if a star performer always does the work.

- Knowledge and ability are concentrated in a few experts. People go along with it because it is easy; they don't have to worry about the job being done right and they don't have to take the time to learn.
- One person or a small group of individuals can become overworked.
- A resentful person might let something fail in order to send a message that they are overworked. If this occurs, you can think of it as its own form of control by the person having the knowledge.

Having individuals who help too much or relying on a star performer who does too much, actually causes a situation where a manager can lose control of a project and the quality of the results. Here is how: reliance on a few key people can result in problems when these key people change positions, become too busy, or the department gets more work and the remaining staff does not have the ability to do the work. These are out-of-control situations in the making because the employees who don't develop skills actually can become a burden on the manager and those who have the knowledge and skills to get the job done.

Example 5: Some individuals don't try to hide their need for control or their controlling behaviors. Often done out in the open, without regard for the feelings or the needs of others, demanding and controlling behaviors do not inspire trust or loyalty from others. Here is a key example:

> A manager, trying to make sure his entire department's work was done for the month, kept the staff working late on the last day of the month. In this situation there was a shortage of personnel and some staff members were in need of training. The volume of work was increasing month by month. When this occurred a few times, employees were willing to help. When it became a regular occurrence, they started complaining. When it became a "scheduled" event that often occurred more than once a month, they became

resentful, saw it as a punishment, and blamed it on poor management. The effect actually reinforced itself; employees had less incentive to try to make their quotas since they had to stay late anyway to make up for a shortage of resources.

The key point we want to make in all of these examples has to do with the crucial difference between:

- times when an individual is controlling the situation and events (positive); and
- times when the individual is trying to control the behaviors and actions of other people (negative).

Even though a company has policies and procedures, and managers have prerogatives, people will follow rules until they reach a point where they feel the rules violate their personal value system. When this happens conflict occurs. Here are a few examples of directions we have heard individuals give others that demonstrate this concept. As you read them,

1. Consider how such statements are controlling.
2. Think about the motives that might be behind them.
3. Consider how motivated you would feel if they were said to you.

- *"You are not getting your work done on time. If this continues, I will have to place you on corrective action."* In this case, the person needed training not threats.
- *"The executives are coming into town. You have to clean your work areas."* Here, there was a disconnect between executives coming to town and cleaning work areas. Were the executives coming to look at the work areas? What the employees needed to know was why the executives were coming to town. Communication was missing.

- *"I need you to tell me when Mary leaves for lunch and comes back."* The boss feels Mary is taking too much time for lunch and is not there when others need her. The point is that others in the department are on a commission plan not on a salary plan so they take shorter lunch breaks. Mary is an hourly employee and is not on a commission plan. The problem here is that the compensation plans are out of sync with the business needs.
- *"The company expects everyone to take vacation; however, one manager expects her staff to check e-mail and voice mail regularly while they are on vacation."* Expects? This points out an issue related to alignment between the manager's value system and the organization's stated policies. There are also potential legal issues that come into play.

Here's an example of a company that espouses values that include "respect for the individual":

> The company gave out little cards with the company mission statement printed on them. The CEO declared that *all employees must be prepared to recite, on demand, the company mission statement and failure could be grounds for termination. Everyone needed to know why the company existed and what its mission was.* The effect on employee morale ranged from apathy to rage. For days people walked around testing each other and reciting the mission statement; some mocking it, others trying hard to memorize it. One individual attached the little card on a paper clip and chain and wore it all day for the world to see. The rule was quickly rescinded, and we will never know what the effects on employee morale and productivity would have been if someone were actually fired for not being able to recite the mission statement on demand.

Why Controlling Behavior Breaks Trust

Making demands can be considered within the scope and privilege of a person with management or leadership responsibilities. However, imposing demands and directives on others actually does nothing to help relationships. When we are controlling and manipulative in any way, people resent it even though they may comply. You have probably heard people say they respect the "office" or the "uniform," not the person in it. People may do what we want, and that may be enough for some managers. But, if we are not people based in our interactions, and if we are not considerate of the impact our decisions have on others:

- It can hinder our ability to attract people to work for us.
- It may create an environment where people bide their time until they find another job.
- Barriers can form between people—they worry about what others are doing and may be doing to them.
- It can lead to a negative reputation for the organization, and make it one where people don't want to work at.

Left unchecked, a person who practices controlling behaviors:

- Intrudes in others' personal lives.
- Ignores a person's right to a reasonable work-life balance.
- Imposes his or her work style on others.
- Upsets the balance of power by creating situations where others cannot say how they truly feel.
- Creates a situation where people become overburdened.
- Lowers productivity because people are focused on self-protection.

Now that we have looked at ways people can exert controlling behaviors over others, often without even realizing it, let's look at factors that contribute to our management style. These factors influence the level of control we exert when we manage ourselves, our personal work, and other people.

Dimensions of Management

Often, what we say gets interpreted, reinterpreted, misinterpreted, and sometimes ignored. It gets changed through personal filters and biases as well. If that is the case, then how do we recognize the management style of the individual we are dealing with, or the contributing factors to their behaving in a controlling way? How can we better understand them? How do we recognize it in ourselves?

One way to look at an individual's style and likelihood for success in an environment is based on the relation of **control** as compared to **knowledge** of the function an individual is working in. Each of us at sometime has had the responsibility to get something done. This control/knowledge approach can be applied to any organizational role, because it reflects a preferred working style as opposed to a management title or a personality type.

Depending on the work environment and the situation at a point in time, different styles will be more effective than others. Our actions are based on two factors.

1. Whether we have a high need or a low need for control.
2. What our level of knowledge, skills, and abilities are in relation to the function we are in.

In a typical work environment we can look at four dimensions of how people manage others around them, and what they mean.

- **Dependent**: Here an individual does not have the skills to know if individuals in his or her group are doing the best job in the best way. This person is dependent on the group for not only getting things done, but how they get done. Having a low need for control, the person may realize that control without knowledge can lead to an antagonized workforce. At the opposite extreme, the person simply doesn't care about the work or how it gets done. In any case, being a dependent manager or peer leaves an individual vulnerable.

- **Controlling**: Here an individual has a driving need to control. The person does not know much about the function or how to get things done, but does want to show he or she is in charge and will do something. What that "something" is no one is sure of, but the person will do something. This may be one of the most problematic or dangerous of the types. Not only will the person antagonize people, but he or she risks looking foolish with a "ready, fire, aim" mentality. The person also may worsen the very problem he or she was brought in to resolve.
- **Micromanager**: This individual knows the function well, often having worked his or her way up through the ranks. The person knows the "how" and "what." The problem is that he or she is often tied to the "this is how it has always been done" syndrome, and tends to be ineffective. This person is the standard against which he or she measures others, but in a different and changing environment this person is not what the standard should be. The individual is stuck focusing on tasks rather than driving results. This often happens when upper management decides to promote from within based on past success. It is also seen when an individual contributor is promoted to manage others.
- **Referent Expert**: This is generally the most effective type of individual. He or she knows the function and can help when needed. The person maintains loose control and allows people the freedom to do their jobs. The person is not only a subject matter expert; he or she also knows how to build strong relationships with others in the workplace. The person focuses on results and can give guidance when necessary. He or she is not threatened by the success of others. The person rewards and promotes people as opportunities arise.

Dimensions of Management

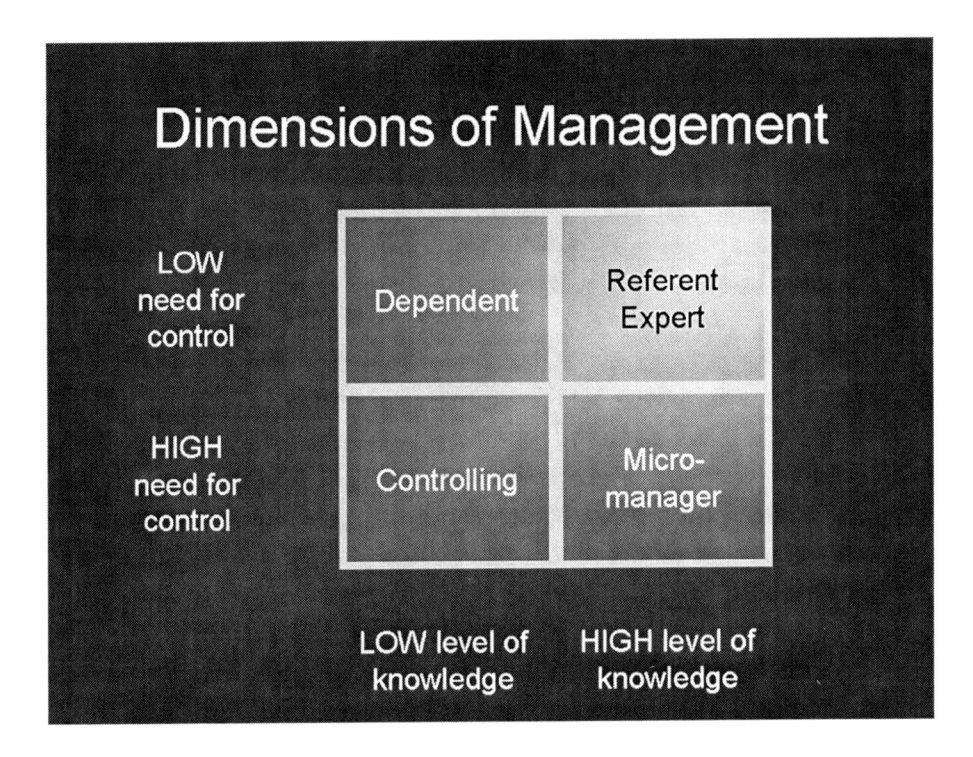

	LOW level of knowledge	HIGH level of knowledge
LOW need for control	Dependent	Referent Expert
HIGH need for control	Controlling	Micro-manager

By considering the different dimensions of management, you may be able to better understand others around you, as well as yourself. As you progress through your career, you may find yourself evolving through these dimensions. The behaviors that are most successful are those that inspire people to have confidence and trust in you. Remember the following...

It is your ability to control the situation, rather than the individual, that will help you achieve success.

Key Points:

- The dimensions of control include:
    - having and gaining control from a self-perspective based on self-interest.
    - maintaining and exercising control from a relationship perspective.

- Positive ways of exercising control help build trust by allowing others to have input in how things get done.

- Negative ways of exercising control result when we go beyond managing a situation to dictating how a person must do things. The result is that individuals become frustrated and demoralized.

- Consequences of controlling behavior include ineffective relationships. Individuals go along because they feel they have no choice. They follow orders and don't take initiative on their own.

- By understanding the "Dimensions of Management" we can more effectively work with others.
    - Dependent managers have no control or knowledge. When working with them they may want you to do everything. Take initiative when working with them.
    - Controlling managers will get something done, but it may not be the right thing. When working with controlling managers present the data and facts to support your goal. Let them make the final decision.
    - Micromanagers want to be involved. They know what to do and how to do it. Offer to help them in other areas.
    - Referent Expert-type managers get things done because they have the knowledge of a job function and also know how to work with individuals to get things done. Collaborate with them.

CHAPTER 10.
THE IMPACT RELATIONSHIPS HAVE ON AN ORGANIZATION'S SUCCESS

Chapter Goals:

- Understand how individuals feel valued/devalued and the impact it has on an organization.

- Understand reasons why individuals feel abandoned.

- Understand how to build relationships.

- Identify fears and how to overcome them.

We All Need to Count on One Another

Work is accomplished through people using tools and processes and that means they are usually creating, sharing, and building new things to help them get their jobs done. Often, they create these tools without knowing or thinking about whether anyone else can or will use them. Problems can occur when the tools that were created are just handed off to other people. Sometimes, the person who created the tools did so based on what he or she knew how to do or based on the knowledge available at the time. The person may have even created inaccuracies in the way the tools or processes work to make it difficult for another person to use them.

Using the following example, we are going to explore a situation that occurred when a manager and two employees discounted the importance of connecting and sharing with each other. Let's meet Gloria and Jeff.

* * *

Scenario:

An employee, Jeff, has left the department he started in and the manager has decided to reallocate the work among the remaining staff until a replacement is found. One employee, Gloria, inherits the complicated budget analysis procedure from Jeff. Jeff created a rather complicated process and spreadsheet to keep track of the department's budget. Jeff did not take time to teach Gloria everything, but has explained the basic process and Gloria has taken careful notes to help her understand since there was no formal documentation. Jeff apologized to Gloria, but said he never had the time to create the documents he planned to. A few weeks later, Gloria discovers that some of the formulas and links in the spreadsheet are inaccurate, which means some of the reports have bad data in them. She contacts Jeff, but he is now too busy in his new job to help her. She takes the problem to her manager.

>Gloria: I have been trying to figure out how the spreadsheet calculations were set up because the report totals do not balance out. I entered everything and ran the report as Jeff taught me, but the numbers don't match up. As Jeff has now gone, do you have some time to go over the process so we can fix the formulas?

>Manager: Jeff didn't have any trouble with the spreadsheet. Didn't he show you how to use it?

>Gloria: He did provide an overview; however, he apparently forgot to explain some important formulas and worksheets in the file. It wasn't until I was adding the recent data and validating my entries that I discovered a number of errors.

>Manager: Well, Gloria, Jeff has been using this process for two years, and he never had any problems with it. You will have to figure it out.

>Gloria: I will see what I can do.

>(Gloria leaves her manager's office and tries to rework the spreadsheet.)

After several hours, Gloria contacts a colleague, Tony, in the Accounting Department, for help. The following week, Gloria's manager calls her into a meeting and wants to know why Gloria had involved another department in her work. Here is the conversation...

Manager: I just received a call from the accounting manager who has asked me to try to cut down on the amount of assistance my department has been requesting from his staff. What is going on, Gloria?

Gloria: I did as you said and tried to fix the spreadsheet, but the figures did not make sense. No one in our department knew how it worked and apparently only Jeff was able to use it. So I called a friend of mine in Accounting to help me. It did take a number of hours spread over a few days, but we corrected the inaccuracies and now we have a spreadsheet that works. I have also documented the process so we can cross train others in the department in case we need a backup.

Manager: There was nothing wrong with that spreadsheet, Gloria. We have used it for a long time. I was not aware that you were unable to carry out the assignment as it was given to you. You also imposed on the Accounting Department.

*(Gloria now recognizes that her manager was **not** concerned with the accuracy of the spreadsheet. As evidenced by the accounting assistance needed, the formulas appear to have been inaccurate.)*

Gloria: I understand, but nonetheless, without the help of my friend, the errors would not have been corrected.

Manager: Fine. But you need to know that it makes all of us look bad when you solicit assistance from other departments. You should know better.

(Gloria's initial reaction is to defend herself, but instead she lets it go.)

Wow! A lot just happened in this brief encounter. When the manager responded by taking the position of "we've never had problems before..." Gloria received a strong message that her manager was abandoning her. Regardless of whether the manager believed Gloria could handle the work or not, the message that was sent was that Gloria was not appreciated. Even though she put in the extra effort in terms of time and energy to fix something, it was not what the manager wanted.

So, Gloria went back to her desk and considered her options. She worked hard and put in a number of hours to fix problems that existed. What do you think Gloria might be thinking right about now?

* * *

Recognize What Just Happened...

This situation is not uncommon. Yet it often goes unrecognized because we are all busy and expect our team members to carry their weight. But all too often we assume that just because one person can do something, others can too—or have the time to figure it out on their own. Or they may be afraid to ask and they do the best they can, hoping no one finds their errors. Let's take a closer look at what really went on.

- Whether Gloria realized it or not, she challenged the manager's effectiveness. The message that came through in the end was that the manager allowed an ineffective, inaccurate process to go on. Or worse, the manager allowed an employee to get away with generating bad data that may have had a negative financial impact on the company.
- Did Jeff sabotage the data? Maybe to make himself and the department look good. Probably not, but how would we even know?
- The implications of a manager basing decisions on inaccurate data are bad enough, but the manager also has to face the possibility that the data could negatively impact other departments and their operations as well. The possibility that this could

eventually become public knowledge could hurt the manager's reputation and her career progression.
- Consider what actions such as these might say about the management and culture of an organization, including its reporting structure. When a person allows personal interest to supersede accomplishing the end result, it can become a standard response to shut out other people and allow self-protection to be the primary focus. Left unchecked, it can become a group social norm.
- The manager did not support Gloria when she needed it. Nor did the manager provide the needed resources.
- The manager did not solicit collaborative input on possible solutions that would help Gloria. Looking good was more important than doing the right thing.

Regardless of the manager's motivation or confidence in Gloria, a potential storm evolved under the surface. And it has to do with *Three Ways People Can be Devalued*...this occurs when the following messages get sent:

- Employees think their manager and others on the team are unwilling to help them. This is compounded if they later find out that someone was, in fact, aware of the situation and could have helped them, but did not.
- Employees feel they are being blamed for something that is not their fault.
- Individuals come under attack for having done what was expected. They were solving a problem, taking initiative, and involving others, but for whatever reason are being blamed for a lack of success.

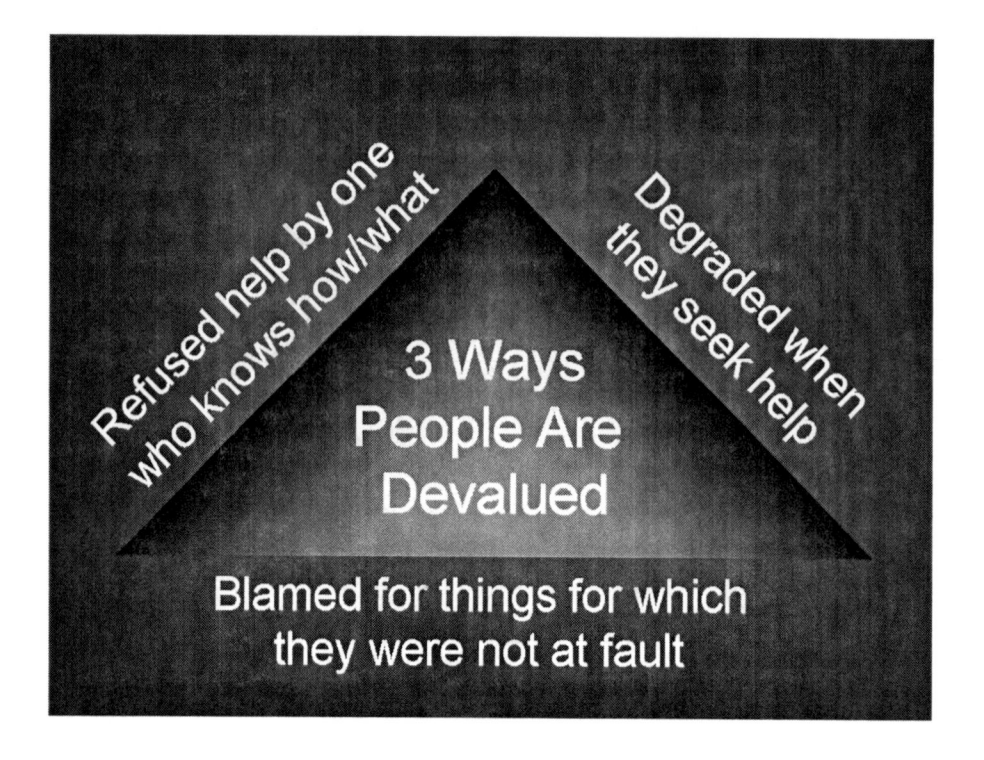

3 Ways People Are Devalued
- Refused help by one who knows how/what
- Degraded when they seek help
- Blamed for things for which they were not at fault

Recognizing the Situation for What it Is...

In this scenario, work had been reallocated due to necessity. The environment was as follows:

- Allocations were not based on individuals' ability to do the job. There were just "handoffs."
- There was no proper planning to identify whether individuals had the knowledge, skills, or abilities to pick up the work.
- Allocation of Jeff's work, which was time sensitive with budget deadlines, was more likely based on who was available because no one else knew how to do the work either. Gloria just happened to be that person.
- Support was not provided when asked for, or when needed.

- There was no discussion of the problem when it was first recognized.

In this situation, the manager had been inattentive and nonresponsive to the amount of effort, expertise, and contributions made by her employees:

- Jeff—had been doing the tasks all along and likely knew how to handle the spreadsheet issues and workarounds. Maybe he had no clue, but tried to create formulas that appeared to provide the correct totals. The data was not derived correctly, but the bottom-line figures were within the budget requirements, so people accepted it as correct.
- Gloria—is struggling due to having incomplete information needed to do the task. She also found a problem that now has to be addressed. The manager was happier when Jeff was working with the numbers, because even though things were wrong, Jeff was able to explain the figures. Therefore, no one questioned the data.
- The rest of the staff—could not provide backup or help. They may have begun to see there were problems with the data, but were not able to understand the scope and impact of the problems. To point out any potential errors may have led to a great deal of work being assigned to individuals who may not have been able to fix them. People were getting by and, as a result, no one wanted to expose the issues or deal with the potential additional work needed to fix the problems. Their point of view was that Jeff had it under control, so why worry. Unfortunately it got handed off to Gloria and that's when issues started to surface.

As for the manager, instead of an offer to help or a willingness to pursue the problem, there was the following:

- Denial that there could be problems with the spreadsheet.
- Handoff of the project to Gloria; handoff of the problem as well.

- Attack on Gloria's self-esteem and competence. The manager should have focused on the problem and fixing it, not attacking the individual.
- Lack of recognition for finding the errors and fixing the problem.
- Blaming Gloria for the situation.

While one might not argue that a manager should have the ability to delegate, delegation is not an abandoning of responsibility. In this scenario, and others you may have witnessed during your own career, there can be an abdication of responsibility and accountability. The manager was more interested in looking good than in doing what was right.

As with all situations, when we are deep in the middle of it all, it is often hard to recognize what is actually happening until the consequences materialize.

Portrait of Gloria's Manager...

Gloria's manager had been with the company a long time. She was focused on doing what it takes to be responsive to leadership.

- Often, she did not question what needed to be done, or how. She just got it done.
- Also, through her interactions at higher levels in the organization, she got to know a lot of senior-level people.
- While she was not seen as an innovator, she was generally seen as someone who followed protocol and process when they existed.

However, by taking a closer look, one sees that in this case, the manager did not delegate—the manager made a handoff. To delegate is to assign responsibility to someone, but delegation does not absolve the manager of the responsibility to follow through and ensure the job gets done—right. Right results accomplished the right way.

Portrait of Gloria...

Gloria was newer to the company and was hired for her skills to get things done. She may have also been hired to bring in a fresh perspective. Having been given this new responsibility, she was also seen as a person who could help the company as it goes through a significant amount of change. She was recognized as someone who could come in and make a difference. Gloria obviously did not always follow protocol, but she got things done.

In a Nutshell...

The message that the manager *wanted* to send to Gloria was: *You are now responsible for the budget process in the department.*

The message received by Gloria was: *Handle it; and oh, by the way, you are on your own. Just get it done and don't make me look bad.*

This is what Gloria did. She tried to work with the budget, and everything was going well until she uncovered errors with what had been done in the past. By doing her job well she found problems that now had to be addressed. *This was not received well in a group that was already short staffed and having problems.*

The Message IS the Action

OK, we know actions speak louder than words. But, think about this... people are typically hired for what they can do, yet how often do we see that the behaviors of individuals in an organization actually *block* the new person from performing to the best of his or her ability. While it can be convenient to blame "the culture," the culture is only what we experience as a result of the individual behaviors of individuals in the organization.

People in positions of authority can abuse their power and manipulate others for their own gain. Unfortunately, any employee will likely feel threatened by the lack of support, and eventually manifest responses that can ultimately lead to complacency, retaliation, aggression, or separation.

If you are a manager, are these the messages you want your behavior to send? If you are an employee, are these the messages you want to hear?

When this type of situation occurs on a regular basis, the following signals are sent:

- The employees may come to think that the quality of their work is unimportant.
- Teams may feel that it is unimportant whether or not they contribute, so they do only enough to get by and do not care all that much if deadlines or goals are missed.
- People may lose the incentive to help one another.

Employees may be thinking to themselves:

- If my manager is not interested in helping me, why should I care about her?
- Why should I work hard when only my manager gets the credit, promotions, and bonuses?
- I am not appreciated here and I am certainly not going to be someone's stepping-stone.
- If they don't care about quality, why should I?

Recognize What You Didn't See...

Managers often don't recognize that their actions can contradict the very values that their companies promote. A manager can abdicate responsibility and abandon his or her people, and can do so either on purpose or accidentally. Regardless of the motivation, there will be consequences. The manager may not be aware of the impact until it is too late, and relationships have been strained or damaged. Consider the list of symptoms and warning signs below, that might indicate that employees do not feel supported in their jobs.

- Employees do not value the manager's decisions.
- Employees work in such a way that the accountability lands back on the manager.

- Employees ask for step-by-step instructions for tasks, sometimes feigning ignorance, and look for ways to set the manager up for failure.
- Employees abandon the manager in any way possible. A common way is not providing supporting data. "I don't know," "You didn't tell me to do that," and "It's not my job" become the ritual responses to everything.
- When potential employees come in for interviews, they hear comments like "This place has problems," "The manager here is having problems," or "All I can say is know what you're getting into before you take a job here."
- Turnover is high.
- Goals, deadlines, and projects slip.
- People who previously worked well together start abandoning each other.

Based on these points, communication suffers. It is common for individuals to begin to see others from a more negative perspective. When someone starts asking questions or is reluctant to make decisions, individuals begin to actively seek opportunities to point out *even more* negatives and question if the person should even be in their role.

Also, consider the effect on other employees in the department who, while not involved in the issues themselves, witness what is happening. It may influence their interactions with the manager. They may begin to question the motivation of others they work with.

Take a Closer Look at How People Abandon Others...

So, how does one break this ugly cycle? To understand how we get into situations like this it is typically necessary to go back and think about how it all began.

Innocently enough, it most often starts from either miscommunication or one individual trying to assert power and control over another. In the case of miscommunication, there is a familiar pattern one can recognize. It typically goes like this.

1. Individuals are generally in agreement on the overall goals, but not the *process* of how to get there.
2. By not agreeing on how processes will be done, misunderstandings arise, which leads to the team having difficulty communicating and achieving its goals.
3. Left uncontrolled, small disagreements around process eventually lead to individuals blaming others for inconsistencies, delays, and failure.
4. Eventually, the focus shifts from *fixing a process* to *fixing a person*. The person becomes isolated and is no longer considered a part of the team. Eventually he or she is abandoned.
5. In such a spiral of escalating negativity, both sides start to interact more cautiously with each other or avoid each other altogether. They make comments to other team members or third parties, and look for ways to discredit each other.
6. If management does not confront the issue, individuals may begin to see management as incompetent and uncaring.

The key to the problem is that the negativity spiral never stops, neither side wins, and this often causes irreparable damage to both parties' careers and relationships. Even if this specific situation gets resolved, the ill will caused by comments to third parties continues to linger for the long term.

Power and Control Relationships within the Negative Spiral

It is common for individuals to work hard to get power, with no intention of taking any risk by letting another individual do anything that may make them look bad. Nor will they allow their employees to get exposure to anyone at a higher level for fear it would reflect negatively on themselves or their group.

> **SIDEBAR**
>
> Most people want to be seen in a positive way and generally want to move their career ahead. Take a look at the behaviors that follow, and check off any you recognize from your past or present interactions with others. Would such behaviors make you feel supported or abandoned?
>
> - People in positions of authority, including your peers, team leads, or managers, become filters and gatekeepers for what gets communicated to others.
> - Individuals scrutinize every detail in what is given to them.
> - People are sensitive, selective, and they censor what gets approved to go to a higher level.
> - Individuals are careful to ensure that they are the ones who take what the group has done to present it to upper management. They are then in the spotlight and have the visibility and recognition, at the expense of their team.
> - What is presented to others, while part of a group effort, may not be representative of the groups' findings, but what the individual feels or believes will sound best to upper management. No one wants to be the messenger when the news is bad. And yes, they do "shoot" messengers.

It is difficult to recover when one falls victim to abandonment. Unfortunately, when it is not stopped early enough for all to recover, the individual team members will have little chance of being seen as valued, no matter how much they contributed. The likelihood they will be set up as the ones to blame if a problem arises is high. And, for some people the only way out is to find another opportunity outside the current organization.

Yet, if one can recognize how and when it is beginning, there are steps one can take to bring it out in the open and end the spiraling behavior patterns. To do that, you need to be able to recognize people who are in the situation, recognize your reactions, and think about some of the insecurities or fears that might be holding you back. The next few sections talk about some of these issues.

Recognize People in These Types of Situations...

As you read, keep the following thought in mind: Reputations are always at stake.

- Someone else in Gloria's situation might have considered the potential consequences of going to a friend in another department and taking up his or her time and potentially impacting their work.
- There are many people who do not feel intimidated to ask other peers or departments for help. However, when you see confident employees take a turn toward insecurity and indecision, a significant change may be in the making.
- On the flip side, some may be to intimidated to ask for help even in their own departments because of how they will be seen. Have you ever been in a situation where you or a coworker approached a more senior-level person—maybe even an expert—to ask for help with a problem? Were you ever made to feel "put down" before the person would even talk to you? Perhaps you asked a question and the person said something like..."Any idiot would know that", in response and only after reasserting superiority did the person actually go on to answer your question. If so,

    - What did you think?
    - How did you feel?
    - What did you do?
    - Did you ever go back to that person for help again?
    - When employees are empowered, they take more risks and solicit more input. You will likely see peer-to-peer coaching going on all around you when employees are happy and engaged in their work. *When you see this type of activity, stop*

and ask what has occurred to cause it. What can you do to help facilitate it?

What Do You Think?

Let's take a closer look at some of the *potential* dynamics around the people who *leave* a department and those who are *left behind*.

- If Jeff's experiences with the manager were like Gloria's, he might not necessarily want to give Gloria any more than the minimum so he could say, "I showed her how to use it." Is this payback to a poor manager? Or is he trying to advise Gloria, figuring this gets us by, so don't question it, just go with it.
- If the spreadsheet is really that complex, difficult, time consuming, or crucial, Jeff gets prestige by being the only one who can do it. Letting Gloria flounder or fail can reinforce Jeff's position and status in the group.
- *This begs the question, would we see a difference in Jeff's actions if he were:*
    - promoted within the same department/division?
    - promoted to a different position with the same company, but in another part of the country?
    - leaving to take a position with another company?
- *How about Gloria, would she have acted differently if she:*
    - were interviewing for a position with another company?
    - had no intention of leaving her company for any number of reasons (close to retirement, good benefits, short commute, and other goals) other than to survive?
    - were hearing rumors of layoffs, downsizing, or reorganization?

SIDEBAR: Those who go and those who are left behind.

Ask yourself, how many talented people have you worked with who have left an organization because of their immediate manager? Have you witnessed any of the following situations before? If so, reflect back on what impact it had on the group.

- People leave, but it is not because they can't do the job. It's because the work environment does not allow their careers to progress.
- People leave because of the relationship or lack of relationship they have with a manager or coworker.
- People leave because they are not recognized for their contributions or their work.

Step-by-Step
Now, let's go back to Gloria's situation, one step at a time...

1. Gloria wanted to come in and do a good job. The budget is a new responsibility for her, and an area where she could grow and develop new skills.
2. In the process of attempting to do a good job she found errors and wanted to fix them.
3. Unfortunately, in this case, Gloria found errors that reflected negatively on her manager.
4. Either the manager's self-doubt or her fear of looking bad to others played a bigger role than the error itself. The manager chose not to confront the errors.
5. The manager also saw the situation as having the potential for her to be seen negatively by peers and upper management.
6. By not helping Gloria, the situation eventually became a bigger issue on a more personal level, than simple errors on a spreadsheet.

7. Gloria didn't take enough time to carefully consider how her manager might view her going outside the department for help. She didn't realize it was about reputations, not just the quality of the work.
8. The manager did not take enough time to consider the consequences of the decision.
9. The result was a relationship that was strained and an environment where fear and anger dominated rather than cooperation and trust

While one would think that someone would tell an individual that exposing the errors in the spreadsheet is the right thing to do, only a few will talk about the consequences of doing so. When individuals are in a position like Gloria, they need to build a network and personal reputation for honesty and hard work. The stronger Gloria's network and reputation are, the harder it will be for anyone to attack her.

Here are some things you might see occurring that will tip you off to a possible situation of abandonment. While you are reading, consider that someone may be acting at a conscious or an unconscious level.

- Employees avoid each other.
- Employees promulgate things such as the "idiocy," "ignorance," or "blindness," of the manager, team, or company.
- Employees make excessive mistakes, some deliberate and some otherwise. And they don't care.
- Employees are gone or unavailable, or available only at inconvenient times.
- Employee arrogance escalates. Employees adopt their own abandoning tactics.
- Employees don't help each other, everyone either sinks or swims.
- Employees may even look for ways to sabotage others' work.

Recognize Your Reactions – What Can You Do

With all of the pressures on us to get more done in less time, it is easy to forget that others are in the same situation. *When you see the signs, here are some things you might do...*

- Step back and look at the bigger picture. Is this one incident or do you see a pattern developing?
- Ask why other's behavior toward you has changed. What is the driving motive?
- Evaluate potential things you can do and the accompanying potential risks and rewards.
- Determine how you can make the best of the situation.
- Have a backup plan. If things don't work, I will . . .

There are also things you do that impact an environment and how individuals respond to you. Give the following self-evaluation a try. Answer the following questions by checking *Always, Often, Seldom, Rarely*.

Evaluate Yourself!

	Always	Often	Seldom	Rarely
Do you just complete activities on your "To Do" list without asking whether they are right, wrong, or could be improved?				
Do you handoff work to others and hope they don't come back to you and ask for help?				
When you delegate work, do you always have to rework it or ask why other people just can't do it right?				
When a problem is brought to you, do you respond by asking others why they can't handle it on their own?				
Are you impatient with people who need you?				
Do you look around and wonder why your coworkers are always so "high maintenance" and always asking for help?				
Do you wonder why no one takes any initiative any more?				
Are you so overloaded that you abandon your staff so your own work will not suffer?				

If you find that you answered *Always* or *Often* to any of the above statements, there is a good chance that there are factors that are contributing to your relationships not being as productive as they could be. The next section will help you recognize some of the fears that contribute to your reactions.

Common Fears...

Is there a particular situation that is causing you to want to avoid problems, forego solutions, and resist taking responsibility? See if one of these fears occasionally intrudes on your thoughts...

- **Fear of failure.** Do you avoid making decisions because you worry they will be the wrong decisions?
- **Fear of losing credibility.** Do you have a concern that if you admit to a problem people will wonder why it took you so long to figure it out or why you let it go on for so long?
- **Fear of being responsible for a poor decision.** Do you make a decision and even after you realize it was not a good decision defend it because you do not want to be seen as making a mistake?
- **Fear of repercussions.** If a mistake is found, do you wonder what the consequences will be when others discover it?
- **Fear of looking incompetent.** Do you avoid hiring the best people? Are you intimidated at the thought of hiring people more competent than yourself? This can be compounded when we add the fear of losing our power or position in our interactions with peers, managers, and subordinates.
- **Fear of loss of authority or power.** If you are seen as making a mistake will it hurt your position and the power that comes from it?

Getting Past the Fear

Getting past the fear begins by understanding where it comes from and evaluating the probability that it will happen. It is easy to have a misperception of another person's authority over us, or the consequences of our actions on others. Our own actions can cause us to give away our power to another person—disempowering ourselves in the process.

Getting past our fears can be as simple as involving others in our analysis of a situation, asking them for input in our alternatives, and keeping them informed of what our actions are. Here are three simple techniques that work.

- **Invite dialog** – Have a conversation! While it is easy to avoid others when things go wrong, it is better to involve them. Help them understand what happened and work together to determine what should be done. This increases the chances of finding the best solution to a problem and helps you get buy-in from those involved. If individuals are part of finding a solution, they are more likely to support the solution. Involve others; start by finding common ground (small areas of agreement) to build on.
- **Empower others** – Enable the team to solve the problem. While you cannot absolve yourself of responsibility, giving others the opportunity to run projects and solve problems gets buy-in and gives individuals the ability to grow and develop new skills.
- **Provide support** – Give people what they need to do the job. Help does not mean do it for them, but it does mean teach them how to do things and provide tools to help them.

Contributing Stressors

There are a number of things that influence what gets done and how it gets done. This can cause conflict, and lead to stress. For example, time deadlines can cause pressure related to which projects have the highest priority, where the most effort should be put, and even more critical, what is the quality vs. time trade-off related to the work. It is important for everyone on the team to understand (not necessarily agree) what will be done and the rewards and consequences that go along with it.

Stress is related to the:

- time an individual has to work on one project vs. the other projects he or she is responsible for.
- skills of each of the team members—if they are the right skills, if they complement each other.
- dependency on others outside of the group's control, but on whom they rely.
- expectations and how they are communicated.
  - It is important to clarify the goals of the project and expectations of the individuals up front and to continually communicate information about them.
  - It is important to have a process to address issues and maintain openness so individuals do not feel the need to hide issues.

Stress also relates to perceived pressure by groups and individuals. It is often related to committing to unrealistic deadlines, which have a negative impact on the quality of the work. It eventually hurts the reputation of the team and individuals who are part of it.

Research has shown that some degree of stress over short periods of time can actually drive individuals to perform at a higher level, but what often happens is that goals right from the start are set as stretch goals and then escalate to near-impossible goals. When this happens, individuals go from wanting to drive harder to giving up altogether. It is also important to keep in mind that stress over a long period of time leads to what is commonly called "burnout." Often individuals may just want to get out of a situation, regardless of the cost.

Recognize What Is at Risk...

Anyone can bring an issue to a manager's attention. Often, it is the person who is trying to make a difference, trying to make things better, trying to make the job easier for everyone. When that individual is put down for bringing up an issue others see what is happening and they lose their desire to contribute. Instead of focusing on what they can accomplish, they look for what they can get out of.

When confronted with something we don't want to accept, it is easy to deny it, require proof, abdicate, abandon, and so on. The way we do it can be instinctive, automatic, calculated, or even unconscious. Often we simply react. But if the effects of the reaction alienate team members, trying to recover from it can be a lost cause. Once trust is broken and people feel powerless or emotionally bruised...

- They become distant.
- They become complacent.
- They react through passivity and inactivity, and in some cases seek revenge.
- They no longer trust.
- They become numb.
- They no longer care.

Three Key Solution Techniques

It is unlikely anyone wants to be abandoned by a supervisor or team. People generally want to be successful and feel they are accomplishing something. So why do we sabotage ourselves? Is it for self-protection? To enhance our self-image? Do we seek some balance of power? The answers to such questions require serious self-reflection. When confronted with a situation where the relationships are not effective, there are some things you can do that will help you work toward a solution.

3 Key Solution Techniques

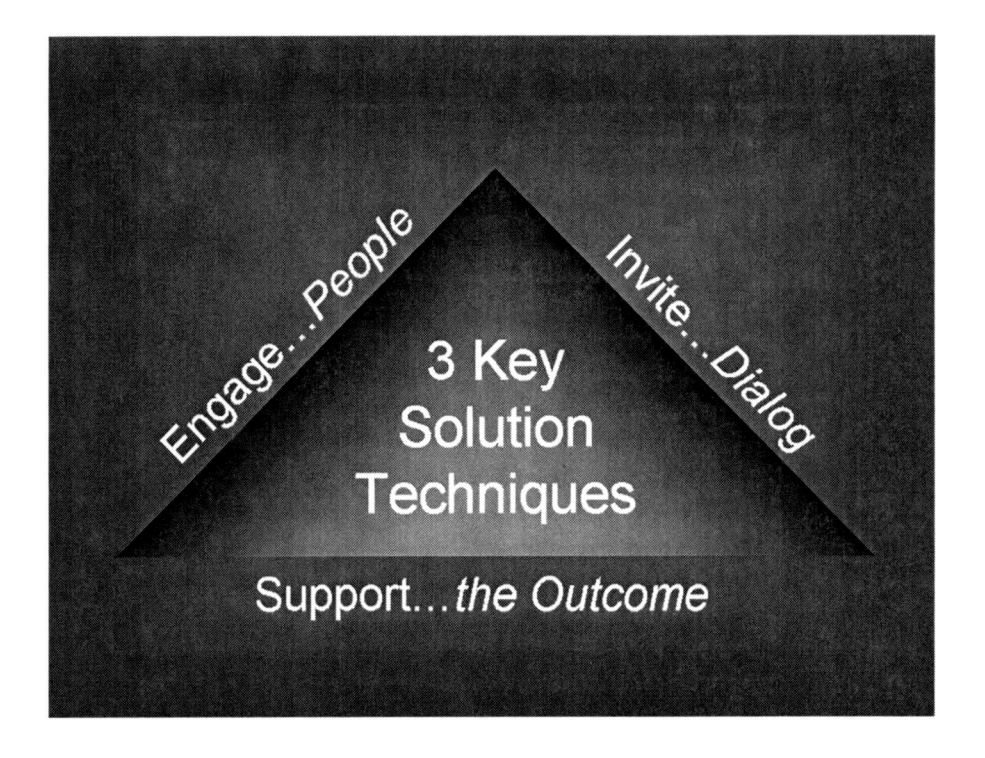

Engage...People
Invite...Dialog
Support...the Outcome

In this chapter's opening scenario, the manager handed off an assignment to Gloria without clarifying expectations or providing support structures. When an issue came up, the result was failure on many levels.

Here is a checklist of recommendations and techniques to help employees feel they have worth and add value to the team and the organization.

- Focus on the outcome, not the bumps along the way.
- Do not expect that just because you can do it, everyone can do it.
  - Remember what it took for you to learn it the first time around.
  - Recall what you learned along the way.
  - Have support systems in place.
  - Monitor regularly and assist when needed.

- Examine the problem from the perspective of the desired end state. Get everyone involved, understand the "whys" and identify what needs to be done. Work to that goal.
    - Understand the situation.
    - Get supporting data and information.
    - Communicate what needs to be done and get everyone involved.
- Look at the circumstances and be proactive.
    - Manage the transition.
    - Provide support.
    - Ensure that knowledge transfer occurs. Don't assume it will happen.
    - Follow up and make sure the processes are working and goals are being achieved.
    - Take ownership and responsibility.
    - Don't abdicate and leave the outcome to chance.
- If a major initiative is being launched, get people involved up front, not just when there is a problem. Make sure they have the right knowledge, skills, and abilities to get things done.
- Show employees you care and are a resource. Let them know how you can help them.
- Be proactive and look for ways to diffuse a situation before it gets to the point of no return. Look for and disarm the triggers that make employees unhappy. Don't chalk it up to their being disgruntled.

In the end, we all want and need the same things—to know we add value and we can count on our team.

When anyone brings you a situation that needs improvement, regardless of whether you are a manager or a peer, ask:

- *How can I best help in solving the problem or aiding in the innovation?*
- *Should I be an advisor, critic, mentor, or should I just do the work myself?*

- *What are the consequences of my approach; will the work get done, will the individuals learn, will the individuals continue to work as a team?*
- *What will success do for us?*
- *Are there contingencies in place?*

And finally, think about this....

Does it really take all that much time to show someone you care?

Key Points:

- Individuals are devalued when:
    - They ask for help and are ignored.
    - They ask for help and are refused.
    - They are put down for asking.
    - They are blamed when things go wrong.

- Overcoming fears begins by recognizing them:
    - Fear of failing.
    - Fear of losing credibility.
    - Fear of being responsible for a poor decision.
    - Fear of repercussions.
    - Fear of looking incompetent.
    - Fear of losing authority or power.

One needs to look beyond the fear to the opportunity. Consider what is the worst that could happen. Build a plan and have contingencies.

- Three key solution techniques:
    - Invite dialog (get communications going to understand the issues).
    - Engage people (try to understand why they have the perspectives they do).
    - Support the outcome (make a decision based on facts and support the decision).

CHAPTER 11.
CREATING AN ATMOSPHERE OF TRUST

Chapter Goals:

- Understand how our past experience impacts how we trust.

- Recognize the Degrees of Trust.

- Be able to analyze and evaluate a situation.

Overheard...
>   *Employee 1 – Don't you trust your coworkers?*
>   *Employee 2 – Oh, I trust them alright. I trust them to stab me in the back!*

REACTING TO THE PAST

People are creatures of habit. Habits can be comfortable and can contribute to the cultural atmosphere of an organization. The cultural atmosphere can cause people to work together for good or ill will. Within any culture, people often build relationships based on how they perceive the motivations of others, and how they see themselves interacting with others. This, in turn, is a reflection of the prevailing attitudes toward trust in an organization, division, or team.

While it looks quite obvious, we invite you to think about how often you have heard people talk about trust. You have probably thought about or even mentioned the following types of behaviors...

- People trusting in the wrong things.
- People trusting in the wrong people.
- People trusting in people for the wrong reasons.
- People trusting things will work out because things always have a way of working out.

You can probably remember times when things went wrong, and you have seen people respond with a wide range of emotions such as being despondent, complacent, passive, defensive, argumentative, aggressive, or abusive, to name a few. You may have watched situations unfold, where people resorted to undermining a person, team, or project based on the relationship or personal motivations. You might have heard about people committing sabotage, creating unnecessary delays, ignoring responsibilities, shifting responsibilities to others, or looking for scapegoats. And, one of the worst things is that you have probably worked closely with some of these people. You may have eventually pegged them as people you cannot trust, or those whom you can trust only up to a certain point. Do you find yourself thinking, "Sad, but true"?

In our work with people, and in our own observations and experiences, we know that we trust different people to different degrees. We also notice that there are three key elements that determine how much we will trust someone. Consider the following illustration:

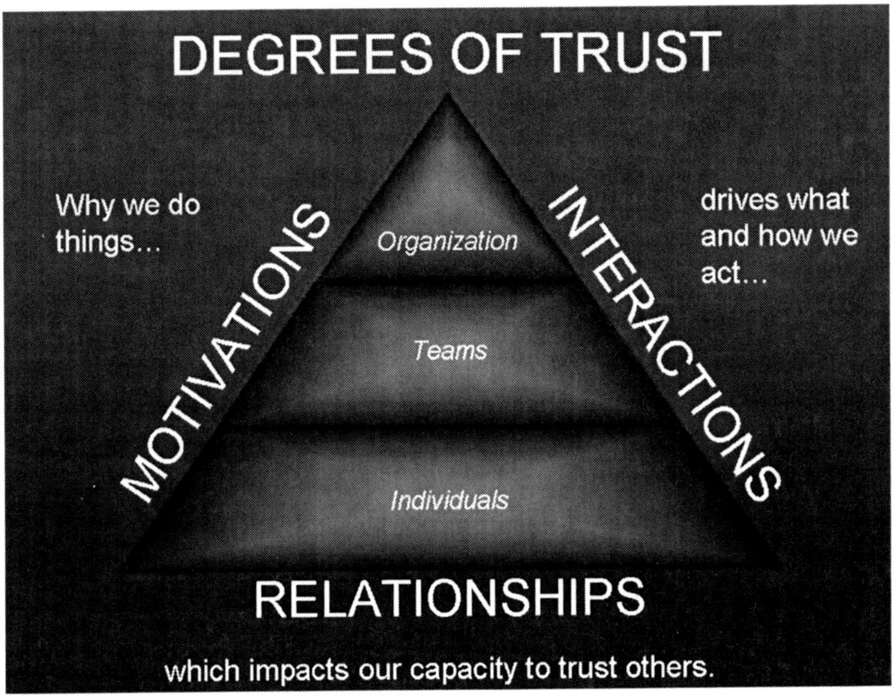
DEGREES OF TRUST
Why we do things...
MOTIVATIONS
Organization
Teams
Individuals
INTERACTIONS
drives what and how we act...
RELATIONSHIPS
which impacts our capacity to trust others.

How much we trust a person, a team, a department, or even an organization depends on...

- How closely our values align with theirs.
- What we believe to be their reasons for their actions.
- What we see them do, in relation to what we hear them say.
- What types of relationships they have formed with others we know.
- How we define trust and truth, with a common frame of reference.
- Shared experiences.

Example

Here are a few situations where you have probably seen this in action.

- Trusting a manager to support you when you make a mistake, but instead the manager distances himself or herself from you. Or worse, isolates you from the group or takes work away from you and leaves you with busy work.
- Trusting that the "system" or "organization" will work it out. This is similar to trusting the system to aid and protect you.
- Trusting yourself or your team to meet a deadline or goal, but obstacles are put in your way.

It makes one ask "who can be trusted?" The organization? Leadership? Peers? Yet, the consequences of not being able to trust others results in our becoming conditioned to look for backstabbing and attacks, so we spend a lot of time dwelling on the negative instead of the positive. If this occurs, you need to ask yourself if you are taking it to extremes and going down the path of mistrusting others. By default it becomes safer and easier not to trust anyone. Take a look at the following and try to gauge where you fit on the trust scale.

How Do You Rate Yourself?

Ask yourself how often you think about the following. Put a check in the box that is most accurate.

	Always	Often	Seldom	Never
You expect some person, manager, or group to mess up, so you do a lot of extra cover-up work to protect yourself.				
You ask yourself, "What are they going to do to me next?"				
You don't have any support from those you work with.				
You feel everyone is working toward the wrong goals.				

	Always	Often	Seldom	Never
You believe the policies, processes, and controls are in place to protect the "chiefs" but not the "little guy."				
You see people deceiving others and not seeing any consequences for their behaviors.				
You accept that when people tell you little white lies, it is part of the normal course of doing business.				
You break a small rule just because you have seen others get away with it or you think you can.				
You can't trust the solutions that are being proposed.				
You can't trust the people who are proposing the solution.				
You prefer to communicate in writing and e-mail as opposed to having face-to-face meetings or having interpersonal conversations.				
You have no confidence things will get better.				

If you have more answers in the "Always" or "Often" boxes than you do in the "Seldom" or "Never" boxes, then you may be getting stuck in a spiral of mistrust.

If you find yourself thinking these things sometimes or even a great deal of the time, *you are not alone!* You may find yourself taking steps to protect yourself, even when the probability of something bad happening is low. Unfortunately, we don't always think about the cost to us in terms of time, peace of mind, and even our own confidence.

How Did We Get Here?

That's a hard question, with many twists and turns. Let's look at a simple, working definition of trust...

Trust... is the sharing of feelings and information with others. We open up to them and share information, experiences, and opinions, hoping that sharing will bring us closer to the persons we share with, and that they may have some ideas or offer to help us in some way.

There is risk in sharing...

- because what we share may at some point be used against us.
- because what we share may not be used in the way we intended.
- because we open up to other people who may interpret what we say differently than what we mean.

We evaluate "risk" before sharing...

- We tend to look at who we are sharing with and we try to understand how the person will use what we share.
- We may consider possible alternatives. However, if we shared something in confidence with someone in the past and that person betrayed our trust by breaking our confidence, it would be difficult to regain the trust we had.
- When we feel we can be deceived, hurt, or used, our level of sharing significantly drops because we are more conscious of the fact that any information we share may be used against us.
- We look for ways that someone might be trying to:
  – manipulate us...

- take advantage of us...
- criticize us...
- impose on our time, good nature...

But the consequences are that...

- We may take our past experiences that did not go well and project them into new situations.
- We may feel that if we were hurt before, we will be hurt again, so we avoid anything or anyone associated with the prior experience.
- We see a pattern of hurtful behaviors and consequences, so we seek to protect ourselves, even when we are not in harm's way.

But What Can We Do?

The question is what can you do when you work in a department or organization that has a culture that causes people to not trust, or to get away with openly deceiving others? Clearly, you cannot blindly trust everyone, because some people are not trustworthy. You can get hurt. Clearly, you cannot mistrust everyone, because most people you have working and personal relationships with are trustworthy. With trust you benefit by having the ability to accomplish more and in a less stressful way. However, it is hard to avoid the trap of accepting a bad culture, doing what everyone else does, and responding the way everyone else responds. In some organizations, mistrust grows, and the environment becomes painful to work in.

In a painful environment, things don't change unless people change, and people don't change unless they see a benefit to changing. If you want things to be better, you have to break the cycle of mistrust. And the way to do it is by taking risks. It is not an easy thing to do. Often, it is a scary thing to do, especially since we can be "punished" for trying. Remember once one becomes accustomed to covering one's tracks and protecting oneself it becomes a habit. Over time, habits become easy to live with even when they are distractions from getting our work done.

If we can break the cycle of mistrust, the consequences are better relationships all around. As we begin to act and respond by looking for ways to trust others, most of them will likely respond in kind. Recall that earlier in the book we talked about things that build and destroy trust. Let's review them again and then go through typical situations to see how our choice of actions can either build or destroy trust.

Trust Triad:
"When I have confidence in someone, then I have less fear of the consequences, I am willing to risk more in the relationship, which then builds confidence, reduces fear, and allows me to accomplish more."

Three Trust Builders:
Being Honest, Validating Others, Accepting Risk Collectively.

Three Trust Destroyers:
Manipulation, Bad Boundaries, Destructive Criticism.

As you look at the situations below, think about situations you have encountered that were similar, and ask yourself the following questions:

1. What do you think is the motivation?
2. How do you think the individual will interact with others?
3. How do you think the relationship will develop?

Situation:	
A manager or coworker is competitive.	
Choice That Builds Trust in the Relationship...	Choice That Destroys Trust in the Relationship...
Seeking challenging projects to improve him or herself and their employees so that everyone benefits.	Being competitive with employees so that the manager looks good but the employees look bad.

Situation:	
A coworker submits a final project on behalf of the entire team.	
Choice That Builds Trust in the Relationship...	Choice That Destroys Trust in the Relationship...
Providing visibility for the entire team, so that all individuals can get recognition for the work they did.	Gaining personal visibility by minimizing or neglecting others' contributions. Taking personal credit for the team's work.

Situation:	
A manager hires a new employee who is more qualified than the manager.	
Choice That Builds Trust in the Relationship...	Choice That Destroys Trust in the Relationship...
Allowing the employee to have experiences to learn and grow, making the entire team more successful. Recognizing the employee has skills, but also helping him or her to become acclimated to the new culture.	Holding the employee back because the manager is threatened by the new employee's skills and abilities. For example, the manager wants the person to focus only on a specific area, instead of allowing the individual to utilize his or her full complement of skills to improve not only a specific area, but the organization as a whole.

Situation: A manager has employees who need more flexibility to meet the demands of difficult family situations	
Choice That Builds Trust in the Relationship... Allowing all employees to work their required hours, provided they do not abuse the privilege and they get their work done.	**Choice That Destroys Trust in the Relationship...** Trust in the Relationship... Selective application of policies, or showing favoritism. Hiding behind rules to enforce a personal agenda.

Situation: Employee is faced with a crisis situation at work.	
Choice That Builds Trust in the Relationship... Manager focuses on the crisis. The causes are identified and events are handled. Manager draws others in to help. Afterward, everyone is briefed, and the employees learn from others' feedback.	**Choice That Destroys Trust in the Relationship...** Manager is defensive and seeks to blame others. The crisis is solved, but there are negative consequences for individuals. People may try to find the solution, but they will also try to protect themselves in the process.

Situation: Manager is called to give a reference for another employee. The manager does not want to lose the employee to another department.	
Choice That Builds Trust in the Relationship...	Choice That Destroys Trust in the Relationship...
Focuses on positive contributions the employee can bring to the new job. Highlights strengths the employee can add to the new department. Is truthful in recounting a good image for the employee.	Focuses on some positive, but also some negative areas in hopes the other person won't hire away the employee. Is not untruthful, but conveys a lower image of the employee for selfish reasons.

The prior situations are but a few that demonstrate the following idea. We make a choice based on whether it brings us value immediately or in the future. Many people, however, focus on only the value it brings them personally and immediately, rather than on how it impacts everyone else involved over the long term.

When we are involved in any interaction with others, we naturally consider whether our personal values, filters, and biases are in sync with the group we are part of and we act accordingly. The key is to act with everyone's best interest in mind. Otherwise, people begin to see us as untrustworthy and they become guarded in their interactions with us. This results in lower effectiveness, lower productivity, less job satisfaction, and less satisfaction with the people we work with, not to mention less personal and organizational success. We don't grow and the culture of mistrust builds. We need to consistently seek to create a solution that benefits everyone, and doesn't just protect us. Remember one thing...

Leaders build relationships when they make other people better.

Key Points:

- Our past experience impacts the way we trust. If, in the past, we trusted someone and things worked out well we tend to be more open. If we have been hurt by others in our trust of them we tend to be more reluctant to share and give our true opinion. The key is to understand the situation and how the individuals involved see us. Ask the question, "What is at risk?" if I share what could happen, from both a positive and negative perspective.

- Degrees of Trust determine how much and what we share.
    - Motivations determine why we do things.
    - Interactions drive what and how we act.
    - Relationships impact our capacity to trust others.

- Understanding a situation and what the rewards and risks are helps determine how much to share and how soon. Trust takes time to build.

CHAPTER 12.
EXPECTATIONS AND COMMUNICATION

Chapter Goals:

- Understand the Three Big Relationship Killers.

- Understand the impact of miscommunication.

- Recognize how situations impact behaviors.

- Recognize how to get past the Fear.

A Typical Scenario...

Work is accomplished through the interaction of many people...and that means many personalities have to come together to accomplish a goal. As such, there will always be differences of opinion regarding differing styles of communication, styles of work, and expectations related to the roles individuals are in. It goes without saying that it is important to work with others in ways that build their self-esteem. Unfortunately, it can be easy to miss this important management skill when we are under pressure to perform.

The following scenario explores a situation that occurs when a manager withdraws from an individual team member. It introduces a situation where the manager does not see exactly what is happening, and the team member does not know how to respond. The manager assigns work without setting clear expectations and without understanding what the team member needs. Part of the solution is for the manager to check for understanding to make sure the individual understands what the expectations are. Team members, on the other hand, are going about their work, assuming they are doing what the manager wants, while the manager assumes everyone knows what is expected. However, it is not uncommon for a manager to fall into a pattern of sending unclear messages to other members of the team. Let's meet Rhonda.

* * *

Scenario:
A department manager assigned a high-level project to Rhonda and has asked her to analyze the situation and propose recommendations for the project. After several weeks of investigation and analysis, Rhonda prepares a report outlining her findings, strategy, and recommendations. Then, Rhonda delivers it to the manager on the scheduled due date. In order to proceed with the project, Rhonda needs her manager's feedback on the recommendations and alternatives.

> Rhonda: *I have finished the analysis and my recommendations are in the report. Do you have some time this week to get together to discuss the strategy and alternatives?*
>
> Manager: *Thanks. I don't have time at the moment, but I'll look at it a little later this week and get back to you. Even better, set up something on my calendar for next week and we'll talk about it then.*

(The manager takes the report, and Rhonda goes back to work.)

The following week, Rhonda meets with her manager, again seeking feedback on the analysis. Rhonda wants the manager's input to ensure she is meeting the expectations of her manager and is proceeding on the right path. Rhonda will need to have a decision from management regarding the alternatives and project strategy. The following week Rhonda sets an appointment with her manager, and here is how the conversation goes...

> Rhonda: *Hi. I wanted to follow up on the report I gave you last week. Do you have any suggestions on the preliminary report? I have also taken some time to develop a few ideas regarding how we can moveforward, and I would like to talk about how we can proceed with any changes you feel may be needed.*

> Manager: Well, you know, it's a fairly long report. Can you just highlight your recommendations in a one-page summary for me?

(Rhonda now recognizes that her manager has not read the report, but Rhonda continues with the discussion by opening to the first page of the report.)

> Rhonda: Here on the first two pages you'll find the executive summary of the key findings, alternatives, and recommendations. I can shorten that section to one page for you this afternoon.

> Manager: We'll also need to create a milestone chart.

(Rhonda turns to the next section of the report.)

> Rhonda: Right here, you can see that the next section has a high-level project plan showing the key milestones. These are, of course, subject to change based on the alternative you choose.

> Manager: Well, I have been very busy working on important things and really have not had any time to look at it. I will get back to you.

Now, Rhonda might not be quite sure how to proceed because the manager gave her a deadline for the project and has neither reviewed her results nor made any decisions. The manager has also not provided any support or encouragement since she met with Rhonda. It is obvious she has not even reviewed the report. But more importantly, by telling Rhonda that she was busy working on important things, the manager has devalued Rhonda and minimized her effort on the project.

So, now Rhonda goes back to work and tries to continue on the project. But how do you think Rhonda is feeling right about now?

* * *

Recognize What Just Happened...

This situation may look typical and benign enough. The manager has every right to allocate work to the team, and the team members are expected to perform their responsibilities. On the surface, it can appear that the manager is accomplishing the department objectives, the team members are meeting their schedules and goals, and everyone is doing good work. In fact, the employees may even have excellent performance reviews, and the department may even be showing progress.

Nonetheless, there is a potential problem brewing under the surface. And it has to do with the *Three Big Relationship Killers*...creating a situation where people feel:

- Their work is discounted.
- They are devalued.
- Their concerns are dismissed.

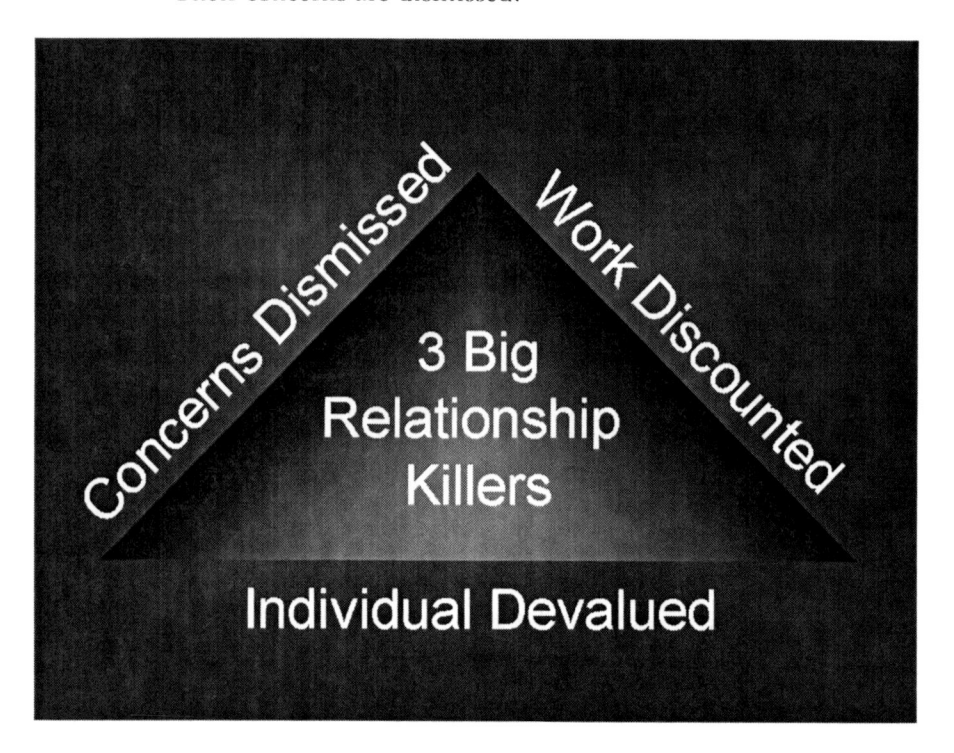

3 Big Relationship Killers
- Concerns Dismissed
- Work Discounted
- Individual Devalued

Recognize the Situation for What It is...

In this situation, the manager had been inattentive and nonresponsive to the amount of effort, expertise, and contributions an employee made. We may often find ourselves in similar situations. The problems start to occur when the manager's behavior is the norm, rather than the exception. In such instances, a manager may not even know that he or she is behaving this way. The problem is that this sends a message to the employee that he or she is not important and that their work is not valued. What subsequently happens is that the quality of the work declines and the relationship between the individual and the manager suffers. Open communication is replaced with limited and defensive communication. Fear grows and trust declines.

Portrait of Two Managers

Less Effective...

Individuals often work hard and are promoted to managers based on what they have done in the past. The challenge, once they become managers, is how to relate and work with others. Take Rhonda's manager in the previous example. Rhonda's manager, while successful, did not relate to the individuals working for her. Rhonda eventually felt the deadlines for getting work done were artificial; the effort she put into her work was minimized, and her manager really did not care about the effort she put into the work. From a feedback perspective there were no negative words, but the actions clearly indicated Rhonda's manager did not think her efforts were very important.

Repeated studies have shown that the number one reason individuals leave an organization is the way they are treated by their immediate manager, not necessarily the organization they work for. In Rhonda's case you can see why. Here her manager was not abusive or directly degrading of her and her work, but the impact of her actions spoke louder than words. Rhonda was not seen as important and her work was not looked at as adding value.

> ### *More Effective...*
>
> Take Suzie, a successful manager. Unlike Rhonda's manager, Suzie focuses on people. She knows the key to getting things done is with the help of others. This does not mean she is easy on others. It means she has learned the strengths and weaknesses of the individuals on her team. She lets individuals know what the real priorities are and has enough self-knowledge to know her own strengths and weaknesses and how they fit in with the team. She prioritizes her people first; to make sure they know what needs to be done and, when possible, offers ideas. She does not know it all, but she knows how to work with her people to get things done. She sets expectations and communicates them to the team.
>
> How does Suzie do this? When a new member joins her team Suzie takes some time to understand the person. In an introductory meeting Suzie wants to know about the person. What the person likes and dislikes, how the person views his or her career direction, what the person hopes to accomplish working in Suzie's group, and what constraints the person may have. A constraint may be a lack of skill, family responsibility outside of work, or the individual's attitude toward work. Suzie also shares the priorities of the group, how she works, what she has found works well, and what some of her constraints are. The key in this meeting is that it sets the framework for the "relationship" as well as the tone for what needs to be done. Expectations are set for how Suzie and the individual will interact.

Successful managers have effective communication skills. They let their people know what they need and are open to conversation about not only what needs to be done, but the "how" and "why" related to it. They treat people as individuals with an understanding of the individual and his or her strengths and weaknesses. They know how to talk to their people to motivate them so they want to do more.

In Rhonda's scenario it would have been better if the manager was clear about setting expectations. For example, she could have set a "first review date" rather than a "deadline" date. If her manager had a number of other priorities that prevented her from reviewing Rhonda's work, she could have asked Rhonda to walk her through it in a summary format. She could have better leveraged her team by letting them know the priorities and deadlines for the group.

A key here is for the manager to decide, up front, whether Rhonda has the capability to get the job done. If so, the manager needs to trust Rhonda to get the job done. The manager needs to make sure expectations are set and are clearly understood. Areas to include are time frames, deadlines, resources—people and technology—quality levels, decision-making authority, and a way to regularly communicate on progress and address issues. The manager needs to be honest about the work and priorities. There needs to be direct dialogue and feedback related to what is good, what is bad, and what needs to be done differently. When miscommunication occurs on a regular basis, employees may begin to do the following:

- They begin to feel they are left out. Team member responses may cause confusion if people begin to question whether they are valued by others. They may also worry about how they are perceived by others. Rather than focusing on the work, they are preoccupied with how others view them.
- They may start to question whether others care about the effort they expend in the department to accomplish the work.
- They may begin to believe they do not add value or contribute to the department. They may question their worth to the organization.
- They may feel that others judge their work arbitrarily, rather than evaluate it on the merit of its supporting facts. Individuals may come to feel that others value only their own goals and do not see anyone else's contributions.

Recognize What You Didn't See...

Managers, supervisors, and even peers, may not realize they are perceived as keeping a cool distance, making arbitrary judgments, or being inattentive. They may not realize that people watch them and even look up to them as role models. There does not have to be a superior-subordinate, command-and-control relationship at all. Considering that the actions of any one person have a direct impact on the performance of the team, distancing postures can cause individuals to disengage from their work. People who are beginning to disengage from their work may show the following symptoms:

- Individuals move *from* seeking out opportunities to engage others *to* being neutral and avoiding people.
- Individuals may start coming in late, leaving early, and not focusing on the job while they are there. Examples include reading the paper, checking the Internet, calling family and friends to catch up on outside activities, and maybe even looking for other employment.
- While at work the tone of an employee's attitude can go from engaging to isolation.
- Individuals do not bring questions or problems to anyone, any longer. They try to avoid people for fear that something bad will happen—more criticism, more work, more insults. Or, they may just feel that no one cares.
- Individuals might do a mediocre or barely adequate job because they feel others do not value their work. In such a case, they may ask themselves why they should put in any real effort if no one appreciates them.
- Individuals may simply throw the job together to meet the deadline and then wait until the manager tells them it is wrong. If feedback is in the form of criticism, individuals may simply ignore it.
- Individuals may even leave the job emotionally. And, eventually walk to another department, or to a competitor.

Take a Closer Look at Why People Create Distance...

Everyone wants the confidence that comes with being on a winning team. However, anyone can get caught up in the trap of expecting that it is enough for people to just do the job. Sometimes, managers and staff alike may take an attitude such as, "If I don't tell you something is wrong, then you are doing OK." While this may work for some team members, not everyone performs well under this management style, especially in environments where it is important to develop others.

For example, some managers approach their jobs from the perspective of "control" and will never praise their employees. They want to control them and keep a level of fear in them. This is unfortunate, but we see it over and over again. It is often from managers who have been with a company for a long time and have moved up the ranks, not always based on skill, but based on longevity and the ability to outlast others.

Ask yourself the following questions, and then come to your own conclusions.

- Did it appear as if the manager expected that Rhonda would be able to continue her project without any input, feedback, or direction?
- Do you think that the manager wanted Rhonda to continue on the project without concrete decisions? Was the manager testing Rhonda? Was there some other factor driving the behavior that had nothing to do with Rhonda or the project?
- Is it possible that the manager was sending signals of disappointment or disapproval by not reviewing the report in any detail? Was it a way of avoiding the conflict of having to confront an employee directly over her long report?
- Do some people, managers or staff, want to victimize others? Or do they themselves feel they are victimized and pass that attitude on?

These are all difficult questions. But analyzing the situation in a little more detail and looking at some of the contributing factors can help us recognize it if it occurs in our workplaces. The key is to understand the motivations of others.

Recognize People in These Types of Situations...

How do people get to a place where they stop interacting with one another and simply give and take orders? How can any of us see it coming and either prevent it or know enough to hold our own against it? Here are some common considerations for when you find yourself on either side of this type of situation.

- First and foremost, it is important to recognize one very important "fact of life." Everyone is different. While this may seem obvious, it is not obvious to everyone. Understand that some people, but not everyone, will interact in the same way you do. In the opening scenario, is it possible that neither Rhonda nor her manager recognized the effect each had on the other?
- Have you seen people who never give feedback to anyone regarding their work? Are employees comfortable in that type of environment where the "absence of rejection" is an automatic "approval"? What about those who aren't? Can they perform to the best of their ability when they don't know how to improve?
- Are there situations where a person makes you feel that "good enough" is never "good enough"?
- Have you known someone who believes that employees need to do only what is asked of them? Did you notice employees not succeeding because they are always on the receiving end of disappointment—never praised or rewarded? Did they seem to detach from the work, their peers, and the organization?

- Have you ever seen someone who always demanded perfection? Did he or she judge everyone's work as inferior, lacking quality, or just wrong? As a result, did employees stop trying?
- Have you seen individuals who are controlling, demanding everything be done according to their own way in order to make sure they, their department, or their work looks good? Were they effective? How many people did they have to replace over the years?
- Was there a time when you knew someone who delegated work and gave little direction, then executed what he or she considered to be "veto" power over the results? Did employees take a vested interest in their work? In the end did other individuals really support them?

If you relate to the situations shown in the preceding questions, then you may be able to recognize when either the manager or the employees are distancing themselves from their work, team, and organization. Company values, goals, and strategies do not matter much to people who have emotionally left their jobs.

Here are some of the things that you might see occurring in the workplace that will tip you off to such situations:

- Employees may avoid interacting directly with others in their own area.
- Conversations become replaced by written memos and summary reports.
- Direct communication is cut off. You may see a proliferation of long, involved e-mails that start with the word "status" and end with the phrase "call if you have questions."
- People may just drop things off on desks without discussion, expecting the recipient will contact them. After all, the employee has "done their part" and handed it off for the next "round."
- Employees may choose not to become involved beyond the minimum. They stop volunteering to help anyone.
- Employees may say things like, "I gave you what you wanted... can I go now?"

If you notice such behaviors occurring or, worse yet, escalating, then you should know that there is a storm brewing. Employees may feel they are only putting in time in exchange for a "paycheck." If people, through their actions, take a posture that employees are in servitude by virtue of their pay check, they may get back only what an employee thinks that "paycheck" is worth. Intervene, question what is going on. Get the issues out in the open and address them.

Recognize that if you are having any of the above feelings...

- You may be disengaging from your job.
- You may be pushing others away from you.
- You may be influencing others to do the same.

Here's the bottom line: employees start a new job being excited, happy, and hopeful that they are meeting their manager's approval. When the environment is negative, the heat of their enthusiasm is chilled. So why do people treat others like this? It is neither complicated nor burdensome to treat people like you would like to be treated. A point worth repeating, "Treat people like you would like to be treated."

SIDEBAR ACTIVITY:

Now let's take a couple of minutes to identify the characteristics of effective managers you have known:

Ask yourself,

1. Who have been the best managers you have ever had?
2. What made them good managers?
3. How were they effective in getting things done?
4. How did they develop and sustain good working relationships with others?

Chances are the best managers you have ever had have been those whom you can relate to. Not necessarily those who have been easy on the work they have given you, but those who were fair, listened when you had an issue, and responded in a direct way without avoiding the question or issue.

Characteristics often mentioned include the manager:
- was someone I could openly talk to.
- cared about me as a person.
- trusted me to do the right thing.
- got things done.
- treated me with respect.

From here the question is to look at yourself:
- How would others describe you?
- What could you be more effective at?
- How do people respond to you when you ask them to do something?
  - Do they understand what you want?
  - Do they agree with what you want done?
  - Do they question why you want them to do something?
  - Do things get completed on time with good results?
  - Do people come to you with questions or just try to figure it out on their own?

> The starting point is evaluating where you are as compared to where you want to be. If your responses tend to indicate people go along with your ideas and openly communicate with you, that's a good start.

Recognize Your Reactions...

With all of the pressures to perform in today's high-performance workplaces, it is easy to find yourself with one or more of the feelings just described. However, there is a big difference between an occasional problem on the job and consistent barriers to performance. Look at the following statements and rate yourself as either: *Always, Often, Seldom,* or *Never.*

Look at Your Work Environment—How Do You Rate Yourself?

	Always	*Often*	*Seldom*	*Never*
Do you avoid interactions with others in your area?				
Do you get annoyed when others have difficulty understanding what you want?				
Do you have to repeat what you say to others a number of times before they "get it"?				
Do you withhold approval from your employees in fear they will ask for more rewards?				
Do you invoke the three relationship killers: making people feel that they or their work is discounted, devalued, and minimized as a way to motivate them?				

	Always	*Often*	*Seldom*	*Never*
Do you avoid giving feedback and having candid discussions?				
Do you prefer to communicate in writing as opposed to having face-to-face meetings and interpersonal conversations?				
Do you find you become engaged in confrontations more than in the past?				

If you find that you answered *Always* or *Often* to three or more of the statements, you may not be as effective as you could be in your relationships. Take a look at the next three sections and you will see possible fears, stresses, or risks that may be triggering those responses in you.

Strategies to Overcome the Fear

Has there ever been a particular situation that caused confusion for you, brought insecurity or anxiety to the job? Have you ever been preoccupied with one of the following fears?

- Fear of making a mistake, or failing in someone else's eyes. Sometimes it is okay to make a mistake as long as you learn from it, and as long as you learn from the others around you. Sometimes getting past a fear is as simple as asking, "What is the worst thing that could happen? What if it did?" If you think you might make a mistake, ask yourself how critical the consequences are, and what you can do to help mitigate them. This is basically looking at a situation and evaluating the potential gain vs. the potential loss. Look at the following to evaluate the risks:
    - Bring in others to get buy-in and a level of understanding. The more others are involved in working with you to

solve a problem, the less the chance that they will reject the solution you (they) come up with. They have been part of the process, which makes it harder to criticize it. Saying something negative about the work reflects negatively back on them and what they did.
- Look for supporters to present your case to. Try to find people who have a common interest. The better you do, the more it helps them.
- Show comparative benchmarks. Look for other similar scenarios and see how they were handled. If the data supports your efforts, reference it in building your case.
- Get expert opinions. Look for individuals who are recognized in the field, quote them, and cite them in building your case.
- Link to similar projects and initiatives to increase the level of support. Helping others helps you.
- Evaluate if you can voice your "fears" as concerns to management. Will what you share be used to help you, or be held against you? If you feel that what you share will come back to haunt you, think twice about sharing with that person.
- Try to gauge the level of risk and the consequences. With that information, you can begin to build a strategy and contingencies. If your original plan does not go as planned, consider your alternatives and how you will transition to them.
- Put the situation in an "if-then" scenario. If I do this then I expect that to happen. What is the best-case scenario, worst-case scenario, most likely outcome, and what are the risks and rewards that go with each of them?
• Fear of losing control of your work, your people, your resources, etc.
- Check it out. Openly ask those around you who can have an impact or can influence these areas to verify your thoughts. Test to see if you are really losing control, or if you just perceive it as such.

- Be decisive. Gather the facts and enough information to support your decisions. Sometimes, one can feel a loss of control when waiting on, or soliciting decisions, from others before taking action. In many cases making a decision today with 80% of the data to support your case is better than waiting until tomorrow for 100% of the data—by then you may have missed your opportunity.
- Identify areas where you have influence. You have probably heard it said more than enough times that "you can't control other people—you can only control your own actions." Even if you are in a position of authority or have management control over others on the team, the most you can do is try to work with people in their decisions and actions. *Influencing others is based on understanding what they value and how it relates to your goals.*

• Fear that your work is not good enough, resulting in a damaged image.
- Unfortunately, our image can be damaged more by what we don't do, than by what we do. Actions do speak louder than words. Inaction speaks as well. Not making a decision is a decision in itself, and your image may suffer if you are perceived as not being able to handle the responsibility of your job.
- Take an iterative approach. Break your work down into manageable pieces and solicit feedback along the way. This will show that you are open to others' input and you are involving other team members. This will increase your likelihood of success.

• Fear of being blamed when it is not your fault.
- This can happen regardless of what you do or don't do. If someone blames you unjustly, you are within your purview to set the record straight. Gather the facts and present your case objectively.

- Fear of humiliation.
  - Unfortunately, we all feel humiliated at one time or another. Usually we are our own toughest critic. In order to improve, we need to take risks, and by doing so we sometimes face humiliation. However, by having continued successes, we decrease the impact of any failures we may face.
- Fear or avoidance of conflict or confrontation.
  - Regarding avoidance, sometimes the more you try to avoid a situation, the worse it is when it finally does occur. Simple examples include leaky pipes or squeaky wheels—eventually they reach a point where you cannot avoid them, and the cost can be greater to fix them when they finally do break. This relates to people and relationships as well. There is a reason why we say things "hit the fan." The earlier the issue is handled, generally the smaller the effort to deal with the problem.
  - Also, think about this. When you handle situations from the standpoint of solving the problem rather than assessing blame, there is less likelihood of a conflict or confrontation.
  - Be proactive, not reactive. By being proactive, you are seen as a catalyst for positive change. Individuals will come to you and share information. By being reactive, you are seen as someone who doesn't have control of the situation.

Getting Past the Fears – Situational Analysis

Use the following chart and think about a situation where you were afraid something negative would happen, but didn't, or where the outcomes were not as bad as you thought they would be. You may find some surprising revelations when you map out some of your experiences. If you can center on a key aspect or identify a trend in things that bother you, you have taken the first step to addressing your apprehension or discomfort.

This table is a framework for evaluating situations you face.

- First, describe the situation.
- Second, look at what could happen if things do not go according to plan—don't just wait until something goes wrong and then decide how to figure it out.
- Third, evaluate the possible alternatives and their feasibility.
- Finally, ask what contingencies might be available should there be a problem.

Evaluate the Level of Criticality

1. Fatal disaster
2. High cost
3. Minor negative impact
4. No negative impact

Situation: Missing a project deadline.
Level of Criticality: High cost.
Possible Alternatives:
• Ask for more resources.
• Extend the project deadline.
• Work overtime.
Contingencies:
• Revisit the level of quality needed.
• Modify scope of the project.

> Situation: A key employee decides to leave the team / organization.
> Level of Criticality: Minor negative impact.
>
> Possible Alternatives:
> - Find out the reason the employee is leaving and see if there is a way to resolve any issues.
> - Hire a temporary external consultant to fill the project role.
> - Have other team members pick up the responsibilities of the individual who is leaving.
>
> Contingencies:
> - Have the person who was on the succession plan step up.
> - Determine if the timeline for the project can be altered.
> - Modify project plans and tasks.

Influencers and Stressors...

Often, we don't see where the stressors come from—they come from so many directions. We often impose many of them on ourselves by our own actions. Can you think of a time when you made a situation worse through your own actions, even though that was not your intention?

Here is a classic example we have witnessed many times, and you may have also seen happen. People are in a group or in a meeting, and someone asks for suggestions. How often have you heard the leader say, "That was a good idea, why don't you handle it"? How often have you heard the other person begrudgingly comply? And if you look back, how often did anyone else make a suggestion after that?

Many stressors are impacted by the way in which we relate to others, and how others relate to the way we treat them. If you answer "yes" to any of the following questions, ask yourself, "Why do I feel that way and what is influencing me?"

- Do you worry when you are accountable for things that are out of your control?
- Do you see mistakes as personal failures?
- Do things have to be perfect for you to feel safe?
- Is it hard for you to adapt to ambiguous, changing situations?
- Do you focus more on the potential risk and loss rather than the reward and gain?

Recognize What Is at Risk...

When we distance ourselves from others, we actually put ourselves at more risk. We lose sight of expectations and become isolated from communications that keep us informed of what needs to be done. Here are three risks that create stressful and unpleasant working relationships.

Manager and Employee Reputations

Employees who feel alienated or intimidated might skate along, doing the minimum and putting in minimal effort. They ask themselves why they should invest a lot of time when they perceive their manager or team leader is disinterested. Unfortunately, the department, as well as the manager, may get a reputation for low-quality work. The team as a whole will be hurt as their perceived effectiveness declines.

Also, if turnover increases, the workload becomes more of a burden on those who remain. The morale of the team and the department will suffer as well. Employees may perceive that there are limited rewards for a job well done. As a result, the level of effort they put into their work decreases.

Project or Production Performance

If distancing and alienation continue, not only will the current quality of team members' work suffer, but the level of their future effort can decline. Employees may come to believe that there is no such thing as doing their "best job" as far as their manager is concerned. *It becomes more of "What can I get away with?"* Therefore, by finding no support, they shift the burden of responsibility away from themselves and let the manager take the consequences. They just follow orders. They would rather not be empowered.

When a manager finds him or herself in such a situation, it can take a lot of time away from the manager's own work and the manager's performance suffers. People may even engage in a ritual of constantly running over to the manager, asking simple questions, seeking validation, checking in. Imagine a manager's day filled with questions his or her staff should handle...*Do you like this, do you want that, should I do it this way, how do you want it, will you sign this, will you approve that*... and so on.

In essence, employees drift away from handling the routine issues on a project and they no longer accumulate a pattern of successes on which they can build. They learn to avoid work. They may even condition themselves to make no decisions or make poor decisions. They may train themselves to work by rote mechanics, and break down when there is no rule to cover the problem.

They learn to become insecure.
They learn to become helpless.

Overburdening Oneself

In the opening scenario of this chapter, we described a manager who was taking a controlling, distancing stance with her employee. Following are specific actions that made the situation worse.

- The manager neither took time to read the report beforehand, nor provided any guidance for Rhonda. The manager saw her time as more valuable than that of her people.
- The manager did not proactively follow up, but waited until Rhonda asked about the status. The manager saw her personal interests take precedence over the work of her employees.
- The manager did not engage Rhonda in the project, but sent a message to Rhonda that she was not an important part of the team. The manager's priorities superseded the team's efforts to meet those priorities.

In our story, the manager pushed Rhonda away through both actions and words. It can be easy to push people away. It takes little effort, and often it is done through nonaction, invalidation, showing displeasure, or giving criticism. When we do these, we are not warming up to people. People no longer feel comfortable around us, and we become seen as unapproachable. We don't let them in.

When a manager makes a habit of showing disappointment or disapproval either through direct action or through inaction, the manager builds a wall. There can also be long-term consequences when the manager suddenly finds that the individuals who can go elsewhere, do so. The manager has lost key performers while those who cannot go anywhere else stay in the department. It also often comes as a surprise when employees leave, and they often simply state they are going for more money or a better opportunity. The real question is, *"Why were they looking in the first place?"*

Solution Checklist – Interact! Warm up!

In this section's scenario, the manager was so inwardly focused that the needs of the employee were ignored. Regardless of whether it was the manager's intention, the result was that the work, and by extension the employee, were both devalued. Here is a checklist of recommendations and techniques to help employees feel they are valued.

- We all have different personalities, but still need to work together. As a manager, one cannot afford to let certain personalities dominate the environment. Focus on goals, roles, and responsibilities. Communicate who is accountable for what. Don't just spend time with those you feel comfortable with.
- Set goals that stretch an employee's abilities and are challenging, but are not so difficult that people just give up. Have a support system—other employees, mentors, and access to information can all be ways to help.
- Look at mistakes for what they are...*learning experiences*. Determine the worst thing that could happen if something goes

wrong. Have contingencies just in case something does not go according to plan.
- Be objective. Recognize that it isn't about what you want, it is about what *your company* needs along with what your *employees* need to develop and grow.
- Show employees and peers that they are valued.
- Encourage them and provide regular feedback. Point out the positive as well as the opportunities to improve. Feedback has the most impact when given at or close to the time an incident happens, not months later.
- Mentor individuals; help them develop the talents and skills they need to be successful so they can help you.
- Let employees know they are welcome to come to you at any time.
- Provide an escalation process for issues that need to be addressed.

In the End, it's Simple.

Honor, respect, and validate everyone. Acknowledge when someone does something well. Celebrate it even if it is small. Share the rewards. Never let your people doubt you care about them or their work. Some simple terms can make a big difference:

> *"I appreciate your work and the effort you put in."*
> *"You work well with others on the team."*
> *"You take a creative approach."*
> *"I like what you have done."*
> *"You may be onto something; help me understand in more detail."*
> *"I am happy that you got it done on time, I know your deadline was short."*

And finally, think about this....

Does it really cost you anything to make people feel good?

Key Points:

- **Keep in mind the Three Big Relationship Killers and how they hurt trust.**
    - **Dismissing an individual's concerns.**
    - **Discounting an individual's work.**
    - **Devaluing an individual's effort and results.**

- Miscommunication is often how relationships and trust deteriorate. Make sure you have outlined a process for communication. Define what the expectations are and how status, questions, and issues will be addressed.

- Relationships are impacted by an individual's behaviors. Often the situation drives how an individual behaves. Behaviors are learned. A key is to understand the situation and ask why an individual would behave a particular way. Ask, "How does what we're involved in impact the relationship?"

- Getting past fear is often simply realizing it exists and understanding why. Ask what is the worst that can happen and, if it does happen, what will I do? Maybe a better question is, what is most likely to happen and how can I make the most of it?

CHAPTER 13.
BREAKING THE CHAINS OF CULTURE

Chapter Goals:

- Understand how to get past the status quo, fear and anxiety, and the tolerance for ambiguity.

- Understand how to get out of the box.

- Understand how to break the chains of culture.

Rules and Rituals

It is said that change will only happen when individuals realize that the pain of staying the same is greater than the pain of change. The chains of culture hold us back from being truly successful because they focus on what has made us successful in the past. Belief in the status quo, fear and anxiety related to taking action, and inaction linked to a tolerance for ambiguity and mediocrity all have a major impact in holding us back from reaching our full potential. We are seen as successful so what we are doing must be right.

BARRIERS: Chains of Culture

Status Quo
Fear & Anxiety
Tolerance for Ambiguity

Corporate rituals, department rituals, and personal rituals—we see them all the time. On the positive side, rituals give us a routine, provide us with a sense of identity, and provide comfort. They provide predictability and some level of security. They are often unquestioned patterns of behavior. No one thinks much of doing anything else different from them. They just seem "right." And besides, everyone else is going along with them. Just think of it from your own perspective. You get up, you follow a typical routine, maybe having breakfast, getting coffee, checking the news, turning on the PC, reading your e-mail, going to lunch, and so on. This seems fine until you have a major event such as a heart attack. When your doctor tells you your weight and eating habits are putting you at risk of dying, you may think about changing. If the message is strong enough and your reasons to live are important enough you will change. If not, you live with the risk and face the consequences.

In organizations the challenge occurs when rituals become barriers and they become propagandized along with other things that define an organization's culture. Rather than being identified as an obstacle to overcome, barriers turn into BUSINESS AS USUAL. They become part of the everyday work routines in an organization. When barriers are raised to a toxic level, people seek support where they can—in groups, in more socializing at work, in more protectionism, in more resistant behaviors, and in distancing themselves from others who have different points of view.

The barriers we have talked about:

- Fixing symptoms rather than solving problems.
- Being impacted by filters and biases in our interactions with others.
- Handing off work, problems, and people issues. Denying problems exist, and delegating the wrong things for the wrong reasons.
- Exercising controlling behaviors, and trying to control people rather than issues.

have an impact at the *individual, team*, and *organizational* levels. When behaviors become ingrained in the culture of the organization, change can seem impossible. In extreme cases it can be seen as a cult mentality. Any attempt at change carries a high risk for those who try.

Rituals are protection on the corporate battlefield. One can say that they followed procedures, so how can they be at fault. The problem when individuals get wrapped up in rituals, tasks, and busywork is that it prevents them from getting the real work done. The consequences are that we create a culture that is ritual based and task driven instead of results oriented. We get lost along the way and may never deal with the real issues or fix the problems that need to be addressed.

When individuals are more concerned with the status quo and fitting in than getting things done, there are usually consequences. Think about the following:

- When people go about their business on "autopilot," executing their job tasks as usual, their focus can shift from the end goal to just following the process. They become trapped into staying within known processes rather than trying to find more effective ways to get things done. They get hung up, doing the same things, in the same ways, and they get the same results they always have. This may have worked in the past, but when the world around you is continually evolving, you must change to be successful in the future. Keep in mind others are always looking to do things better, faster, and cheaper. How will you compete? What is your vision? What does the big picture look like? What is your role in it? These all need to be defined.
- When people focus on fitting in, fitting in becomes the goal. They think I'm OK if I fit in. They just go along with what everyone else is doing even if it is not the best thing to do. In some cases they will stand by or even be involved in doing what they know is wrong. There is no tolerance for diversity of thought. We have all seen the horrible impact and what has happened to some of the largest corporations and corporate leaders when this has occurred. Learn to be aware of what is going on. Remember to look at situations and ask, "What if?"
- When there is an environment of "no tolerance" for differences, individuals are expected to conform and not give their opinions. If you are a manager and you are part of creating or enforcing this type of environment, ask yourself why. What do you have to lose if you let others help you to be more successful? What do you have to gain? Building a network of successful individuals leads to trusting relationships that help make individuals even more successful in the future. If you, on the other hand, are a member of an environment like this and see no chance for change, begin to look for options and a way out. To think, "I only have to put up with this for another ten years before retirement"—is no way to live. Don't hope things will change, take action.

As you have probably heard, seen, or suffered through some of the above, the key is to recognize when individuals are operating in these modes. Try to understand their motivations and determine whether they fit with your values and what you can do about them. Build a personal development plan and take action to move you toward your goals. Don't get stuck with a "that's how it has always been done" mentality.

Rituals and the Status Quo

> ### SIDEBAR – The Pot and the Pot Roast
>
> You have probably heard this story, we're not sure where it originated, but it brings the point across. There was a family party and a husband was watching his wife prepare a pot roast they were going to serve. He noticed his wife cut off both ends of the pot roast before putting it in the roasting pan. He asked why she cut the ends off. She said now that you mention it, I'm not sure. Mama always did it and I believe it has something to do with the way it cooks.
>
> So the husband went and asked his mother-in-law (Mama) why she cut the ends off the pot roast before putting it in the oven. Her response was, that was how Grandma always did it and that was what she taught me to do. I never thought about it, but I believe it has to do with how it cooks.
>
> Then he went to ask Grandma why she cut off the ends of the pot roast. Grandma's response was that she only had a small roasting pan and the pot roast would not fit in it unless she cut the ends off.
>
> The point is, do you really understand why you do what you do? And, do you realize the impact it has on other people, the costs to the business, and the impact on overall results? How much pot roast have you wasted over the years? You may not even know what you have been wasting or doing inefficiently. The key is to be open to questions and look to understand why we do things. Often, we may do them out of habit, rather than reason.

THE STATUS QUO IS SAFE. If we keep the status quo, it does not matter how bad the problem gets. We don't have any more risk than anyone else. Not too much is going to happen to us that doesn't happen to everyone else. And everyone is in the same situation (misery loves company). We're safe in the rituals.

THE STATUS QUO PROVIDES COMFORT. Why do we keep the status quo when change is warranted? The answer is that there is fear and risk that goes with change. We don't know how the change will impact us and we fear the worst.

THE STATUS QUO IS FAMILIAR. Keeping the status quo tempers the fear. It's good enough for everyone else; it is good enough for me. It becomes not only the thing to do, but the reason and possibly the *excuse* to do it. It makes change harder to maneuver through.

So, while the status quo allows individuals to identify and work together, we need to be careful not to let it replace the real reason our organization exists and to not detract from the goals we are trying to accomplish.

3 Sides of the Status Quo

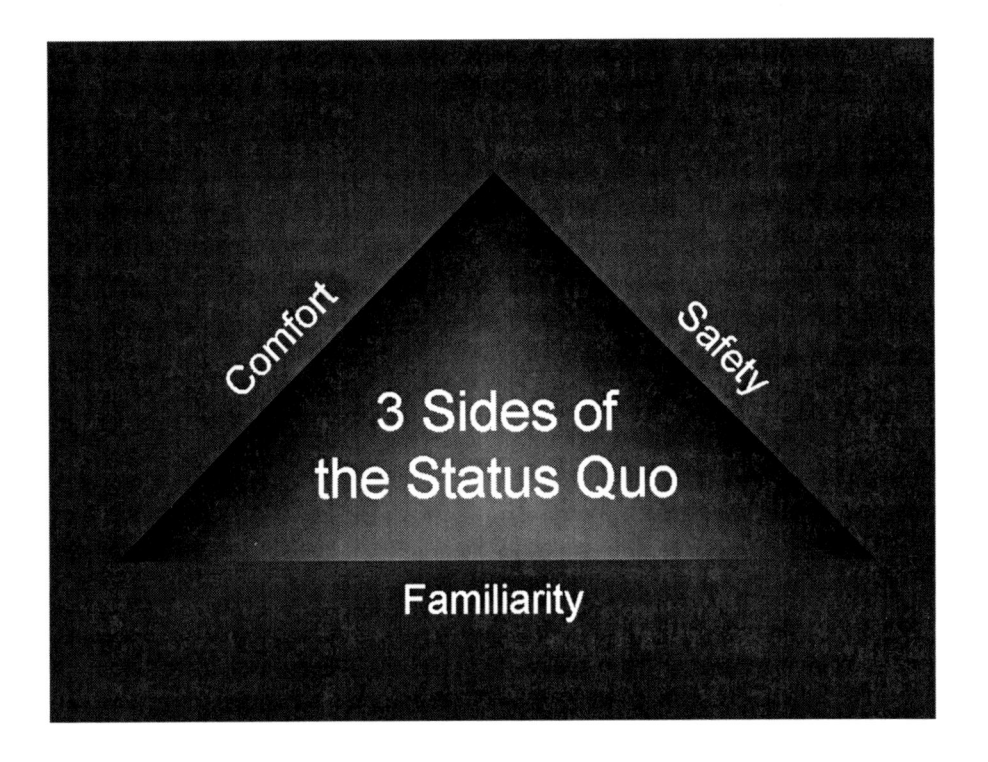

- Comfort
- Safety
- Familiarity

Breaking the Chains of Culture

An organization's culture is driven by a number of factors including how people relate to each other, how they communicate with each other, and how decisions are made. Often the "rules" of the culture and how they are followed are more important than the work itself. Being aware of these factors can help you be more effective in successfully navigating through the organization.

Keeping a balance between achieving your personal goals and playing by the organization's rules becomes the skill you must master. It consists of building the appropriate alliances, presenting your ideas and suggestions in a way to get support from others, and being seen as credible... someone others can count on to help them.

Sometimes, politically motivated and career-driven individuals don't want to openly be seen as allies. They might feel that if you fall out of favor, they will fall out of favor because they associate with you. This further separates individuals in an organization. No longer is it about talent and capability. Individuals fear the consequences of being seen with someone whose stance and opinions are different from the mainstream. They feel they will be judged based on "guilt by association." However, watch how quickly this changes when a former outcast begins to get support and backing behind what they are doing.

The opposite is also true. Think of any leader who once had a position of power and influence and then fell out of favor. Recall how quickly many so-called supporters abandoned that person, even if that person had gone to great lengths to help them in the past. The key is to find and build alliances with those you can rely on, whether times are good or bad.

The chains of culture can be hard to break. Each link in the chain is forged by some ritual that has become ingrained in the culture. Individuals often wrap chains around themselves because it makes them feel safe. They follow procedures, focus on appearances, and go from valuing accomplishments to valuing the rituals themselves more than the accomplishments they have made. They get locked into a narrow way of thinking.

You often hear the term "stuck in a box" and that individuals and organizations are stuck in a box or cannot think outside the box. Individuals and organizations become "boxed" when they stop looking for new ways of doing things. They accept what is and do not try to improve because the status quo is accepted. Trying new and different things is seen as having risk.

BARRIERS: Inside the Status Quo

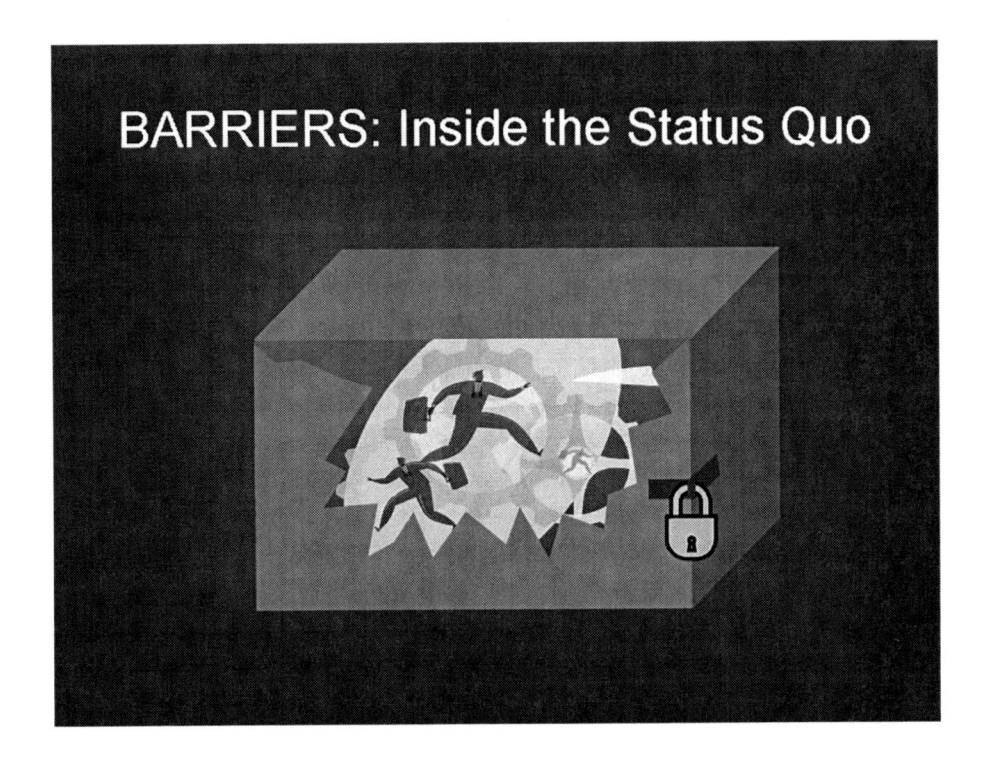

Fear and Anxiety

Earlier we looked at a number of fears that hold us back from being successful;

- Fear of failure
- Fear of punishment
- Fear of embarrassment
- Fear of losing power

These fears and the related anxiety can cause us to get stuck in a box. Here are some examples and consequences of getting stuck in a box:

- Managers and leaders can drive a culture based on the fear of making a mistake. In some organizations, making a mistake is worse than doing nothing at all. Individuals in such cultures live in fear. The penalty for doing the wrong thing or taking the wrong approach can lead to critical consequences. When taken to extremes, individuals will not make a decision for fear of punishment. Individuals are preoccupied with doing what the boss wants (or what they think he or she wants). They can become solely task driven, without being focused on strategies or problem solving. It is easier to do what is "safe," rather than right. Eventually things change, whether externally driven or internally forced by changes in other parts of the organization. It is usually better to be part of making change happen than to be impacted by the change others force on you.

- Organizations that don't change and innovate become obsolete and go away. Even an organization that at one point came up with a new product or service that was seen as valued at the time can fall into the complacency trap. *Making the greatest buggy whips in the world does no good when no one has buggies any more. The pay phone was a great innovation in its day, but with cell phones how many pay phones still exist today?* One can look at the Fortune 500 list from ten years ago and compare it to today. About half the companies on the list back then are no longer here.

- A "me first" environment has been created in many organizations. A reward "the hero" not the team approach has been put in place. *Rewards are seen as getting a piece of the pie. Unfortunately the pie is fixed in size. So, for me to get more—you have to get less.* It's about "me first" or "fill my needs first" before I can have any thoughts about how others are affected. If your organization still rewards this way, ask why. Is it effective? What message does it send? What barriers does it build?

- In the past, individuals could easily spend their entire career with one organization. Today this is not likely. In the past being the dedicated "company man" doing whatever the organization wanted would keep you in a job for life and lead to success. Today individuals need to focus on continually learning and building skills related to their career development and not just focus on a company's culture. Having and voicing an opinion becomes more important. Holding back is seen as ineffective and uncooperative.

When one grows up in a culture, it is natural to accept the status quo. When one has spent a great deal of time in a given work environment, the risk of taking a stance or making a change may seem too great. If an individual's job evolved in that environment, it may be that the individual has limited career choices. The person may feel stuck. The person may do things he or she does not believe are correct. Peer pressure can cause one to conform to the status quo. For the individual, it's survival, and in that environment it may be how the person got to where he or she is.

- If a person has been in only one organization, he or she may not know the difference and naturally expects things to happen the way they have always happened.
- For those who have worked in multiple organizations, they may see that the environment is not the most productive, but they understand how to work it for their personal success or to meet their own agenda. The organization and its needs become secondary.

Tolerance for Ambiguity

- Sometimes we are so busy we don't have time to deal with the consequences of getting out of our box. Even though we feel we are not at our optimum, we keep on going because that is what the culture expects. We overlook the errors of others and accept secondary quality.
- We learn that getting by is good enough. We can function at less than a high level of proficiency with no conflicts or controversy. When we go outside the box and start to test our skills and abilities, we draw attention and others may question our motives. It is easier to just get along. As a result we do not set our goals to stretch our skills and build our abilities. We accept mediocre performance because it is easier than

pointing out a problem and dealing with the issues related to it.
- Going outside the box means going outside our established support system. We may not want to take the risk. Finding or building a new support system can be difficult. It may even contradict what our current support system espouses.
- Tolerating ambiguity can make it easier to give into cultural pressures rather than to try to make changes. Generally, the longer individuals have been on a team or within an organization the harder it is to see things from a different point of view, much less try to change something. People feel compelled to live in the box rather than think outside it.

Why it Breaks Trust

When we are locked within a certain paradigm, even in the face of change and innovation, we can become blind to opportunities and innovation, and we may limit ourselves to what we already know and understand. When one relies on the status quo, it leads to the following possible effects on us and those around us:

- Disempowers individuals.
- Individuals become biased and prejudiced.
- Individuals block out opinions and perspectives that differ from their own.
- There is the chance of creating negative peer groups with their own social norms.
- There can be resulting negative influences that demoralize and isolate individuals from the others they need to be successful.

If one is successful in objectively looking at the rituals that lock us into a rigid, regimented way of thinking, we can begin to see options for success that we otherwise might dismiss or not even think to consider. The following presents a perspective on how you might handle yourself in a rigid environment.

When this type of environment exists, ask how individuals' behaviors do not support the organization's goals and values.

1. Step back and review what your organizations' goals and values are, and recall why your organization exists in the first place. Differentiate between what is said and what is acted on.

2. Ask how your behaviors are supporting the goals you are trying to accomplish as well as the values you are trying to live by.

3. Consider how the current status quo helps support the organization's reason for being, and how the current status quo is helping or hindering the organization from achieving its goals in the future.

4. Build a case with facts. How well is the organization performing? Are you reaching your personal goals? Are you accomplishing your short and long term objectives? Why? Why not?

As an individual, look to learn and build your reasons for doing things and making changes based on how the organization's goals will be met. Look for small successes to build momentum and allies who can help you. Some of this may have to be done by involving only a few people in the beginning until you are clear on what you are trying to accomplish. As you gain more information and support, there will be times when you may need to bring in a larger group, and promote your ideas publicly to gain more support and assistance. The key is to know whom you can count on and when to apply the appropriate strategy.

As a manager who is working in this type of environment, it is important to understand your people and their tolerance for risk and change. Talk to your people and get to know them. Who are the ones willing to make things happen? Who are the ones that have the capacity to make things happen?

George Vukotich Ph. D.

Finally think about this...

It is the individuals who recognize there are chains holding them back that have the power to make a difference. What effort does it take to break those chains?

Key Points:

- Barriers keep us in a box. Recognizing and understanding what barriers are keeping us from accomplishing our goals is the beginning in determining how to deal with and overcome them.

- The three factors that reinforce the status quo:

    - The status quo is safe. We cannot be blamed if we just do what we have always done. The problem is that change and innovation never take place.

    - The status quo provides comfort. If everyone is going along and we want to be like everyone else, we just do what they do. We are accepted as one of the group. The problem is that things change and maintaining the status quo eventually leads to a lack of competitiveness, not meeting customers' needs, and not being able to change with a changing global environment.

    - The status quo is familiar. We know what to expect and we become comfortable, but continuing to be competitive requires learning and growth.

- Getting stuck in the box happens when:

    - We work in a culture based on a fear of making mistakes. The penalty for doing something wrong is greater than the reward for taking a risk.

    - We get comfortable with how things are and so does everyone else.

    - We fear doing something different.

- Getting out of the box allows you to reach new goals and develop new skills. Building strong relationships and getting support for initiatives helps open the door to new opportunities. Showing others what is in it for them and why they should support you is key.

SOME FINAL THOUGHTS...

We have shared with you a number of situations we have seen, and provided techniques that have helped individuals identify and effectively deal with similar difficult situations. We have shown some of the risks involved, as well as potential consequences of allowing the barriers to become entrenched in both personal and work environments.

The barriers we have discussed are common and typical obstacles to forming good relationships based on trust. We have seen these barriers over and over again in both personal and professional interactions. Often we have seen them go unnoticed or just ignored until there are consequences that negatively impact the relationships and the quality of work. Often once trust is broken it is difficult to repair. We have provided some insight into how to recognize when people are using behaviors that can impact trust, and how situations can evolve and escalate.

We have also demonstrated that when barriers are not dealt with early on, they worsen and affect people at the individual level, group level, and organizational level. Barriers create a framework that makes it difficult for individuals to work together, they create a high level of stress and frustration, and they often push people out of an organization. Whether they leave physically or just check out mentally or emotionally, you may no longer have their buy-in, commitment, or their trust.

To manage any type of relationship, you need to first look at what motivates you, what your goals and objectives are, and what your plan is for reaching them. The second thing is to look at and understand how your actions impact the people around you. You can see the effects your actions have on other people in your relationships as you watch their behavior. You will begin to notice if they start to change their behavior toward you...

either to trust you more or to pull away. That is when you need to question yourself and evaluate what the impact of their changed behavior is on the goals you are trying to achieve.

It is important to recognize why you and others do the things you do. Sound relationships begin and grow when you truly understand why a person is taking a particular position or responding in a particular way. Be objective when you listen to another person's point of view and try to see things from his or her perspective.

Finally, keep in mind that depending on the relationship, some individuals may say things just to go along with you. However, it is their behaviors that will define how much they support you and the level of trust between you. What they share with you will depend on how they experienced and interpreted your early reaction to what they said or did, when the relationship was just forming.

Problems in any relationship worsen when one person unintentionally assigns a value to the other person's needs. Try to put yourself in the other person's place and understand what influences or motivates them. Try to be sensitive to their personal and work style. Also, understand there may be other needs beyond what they are revealing to you and be sensitive to the fact that they may want to keep issues private.

In the end, it's all about how you manage your relationships.

- It's about knowing yourself and what you value.
- It's about knowing others and dealing with issues that come up along the way.
- It's about understanding your collective strengths and how to leverage them in achieving your goals.

The key to successful personal and work relationships is being able to recognize and build on common beliefs and values. Use the techniques you have learned in this book to build the type of trusting relationships you want. Look for and break the chains in your culture that are working against you to block your progress and hold you back from what you want to achieve individually and collectively.

Three Keys to Outstanding Relationships

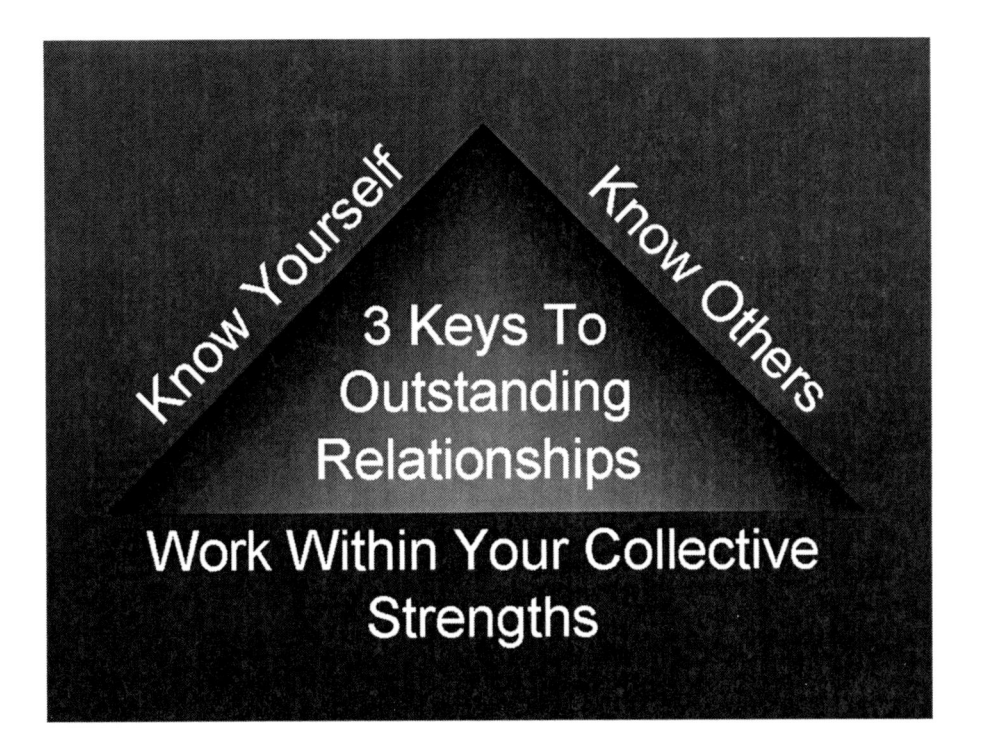

Know Yourself — **Know Others**
3 Keys To Outstanding Relationships
Work Within Your Collective Strengths

You Can Make a Difference